www.milestonechurch.com
ISBN: 978-1-954961-10-4
Printed in the United States.

UNSHAKABLE

FINDING SAFETY & SECURITY IN THE KINGDOM OF GOD

HERE'S
THE PLAN

1. Grow closer to God as you understand and study His Word.

2. Study the intro weeks individually. Study weeks 1-8 with a group.

3. Discover how the Kingdom of God leads to an unshakable life.

TIP: Throughout the book you'll find arrows ◀▶. Some will have symbols or dotted lines and others will be blank. These arrows exist to help you connect references mentioned in the main bodies of text with information and Scripture in the margins. All you have to do is match the symbols or follow the dotted lines.

HOW THIS
GUIDE WORKS

READ THE CHAPTER
- Concept
- Passage in Context
- What Does This Mean for Us?
- What Do I Do with This?

INTERACT WITH THE CONCEPTS
- Take notes in the margins.
- Write out answers to the questions.
- Memorize the weekly verse.
  (Cards located in the back of this guide.)

TALK ABOUT IT WITH YOUR GROUP
Starting with Week One:
"WHY DOES IT MATTER IF GOD IS STILL ON
HIS THRONE?"

CONTENTS

WHAT IS THE *KINGDOM OF GOD?*

PASSAGE:
MARK 1:14b-15

MEMORY VERSE:
PSALM 62:1-2

PAGES 1-14

CONCEPT

Have you ever wondered why so many famous stories follow the same pattern?

- **A fairy tale featuring kings and princesses**
- **A fantasy with knights and dragons**
- **A western with a threatened family, outlaws, and a brave lawman**
- **A science fiction story from a long time ago, in a galaxy far, far away**
- **One of the multitude of superhero stories**
- **The same Hallmark movie they keep making over and over**

The primary plot is the same. It feels like everything is shaking. Something in our world is deeply broken. Our future is in doubt. We are afraid. Where can we turn for help? We wait and look for someone of great character to come and rescue us.

These stories resonate because this is the human experience.

We know something is not right in the world.

Just when it feels like we get our lives right where we want them...things start to change. Life begins to shake. Relationships struggle. Sickness arrives unexpectedly. A financial crisis develops.

Sound familiar? You are not alone.

If we're really honest, we all know we do not have the power to fix it. Even if we could, we know it's only a matter of time before things start shaking again.

There is a simple explanation for this universal human experience—this is the reality of the world we live in. But there is **good news** (a very important phrase we will come back to). These stories persist because there is someone out there who is watching, who sees us when we shake, and who will rescue us. And unlike us, His future is never in doubt. He sits on a throne that cannot be shaken.

No matter what happens in our economy, whatever the weather brings, how the election turns out, what the doctor's report says, and even who lives and who dies... He's still on His throne.

> No matter what happens in our economy, whatever the weather brings, how the election turns out, what the doctor's report says, and even who lives and who dies . . . He's still on His throne.

This changes the way we live. The writer of Hebrews explains it this way in chapter 12 verse 28:

> *Therefore, since we are receiving a kingdom that cannot be shaken, let us be thankful, and so worship God acceptably with reverence and awe...*

You might be wondering, *What's the deal with a kingdom? What does that mean? Are we back to talking about stories?*

In the ancient world, people related to each other in tribes. These were your people. You shared a common story and an identity. Every tribe had a god they looked to for protection and provision. These gods were capricious— you never knew what to expect. They would get angry and punish you. Sometimes they would ignore you.

You didn't always know where they were, or *if* they were, on their throne. But they were your source of help, so you did everything you could to appease them.

You never really knew how to make them happy, but if you could, then you could expect them to make you happy.

When most people hear this explanation of history, their first thought is, *Those people were so primitive and superstitious.* But the truth is, we're more like them than we admit.

We just look to different gods to make us happy. In our modern world, we treat whatever we love most as our "tribal god." It may be your career, it may be your soulmate, it may be your kids and their success, or it may be your personal freedoms. The goal is the same: *If I can get it just right, then I'll be happy.* When things start to shake, and eventually they always do, we look to these things for peace and comfort.

This brings us back to Hebrews 12. The God of the Bible is saying to us, "My Kingdom can't be shaken. I'm not like your tribal gods. I'm always on My throne."

Bible scholars tell us that this idea of "the Kingdom of God" is one of the biggest themes in the entire Bible. You may have never thought about it. But it's good news. In fact, it's *the* good news Jesus came to bring.

It's hard for us to grasp because when we hear that phrase we think of a place—maybe it's an image of a castle or maybe it's your concept of heaven. But when the Bible uses the phrase "the Kingdom of God," it can best be understood as "the rule and reign of God."

Everything is how God wants it to be.

Once you know how to receive this, it changes everything. It makes you thankful. It makes you want to worship with reverence and awe. In Him, we can be unshakable.

PASSAGE

IN CONTEXT

Have you ever thought about how Jesus started His public ministry?

You may remember the last thing He told His disciples before He left. We call it the Great Commission. In Matthew 28:18-20, He sent them into the world to carry out His purpose: to make disciples, to baptize them, and to teach them everything He had commanded. He promised to be with them (and us) always, even until the end of the age.

But how did it start? What was the first thing He said?

These are great question. Unlike Matthew and Luke, the Gospel of Mark skips any details about Jesus' birth, His family, or His origin story. It jumps right into His ministry.

Mark tells us this is the beginning of the good news (there's that phrase again) about Jesus the Messiah, the Son of God, as it was written by the prophet Isaiah.

Why does Mark go back hundreds of years to the prophet Isaiah? And why does Isaiah talk about God preparing the way for the Lord? And then why does Mark think John the Baptist was fulfilling this ancient plan?

It all goes back to this idea of the Kingdom. The Messiah was God's promised servant who would bring back the rule and reign of God. He was the one God's people were waiting for to make everything right.

A messiah is someone who comes to save the people. When we tell stories of heroes, victorious kings, and superheroes, they're all different versions of a messiah.

The Messiah is sent by God to restore what was broken. This is also why Mark tells us that John points to Jesus as the one we've been waiting for, the Father lovingly affirms His Son at His baptism, and then Jesus goes to deal with Satan in the desert. Satan is the fraudulent ruler of a rival kingdom. Jesus confronts him directly before He says anything to the people, and He would continue to deal with him during His ministry.

All of this sets the stage for what Jesus does next. Watch carefully. He does not say, "I came to start Christianity," or "I came to give you religious principles so you could earn your way into peace with God."

He says the same thing He would tell His first disciples to say when He sent them out.

Read Mark 1:14b-15 on page 8.

Read Mark 1:14b-15 on page 8.

MARK 1:9-11

9 At that time Jesus came from Nazareth in Galilee and was baptized by John in the Jordan. 10 Just as Jesus was coming up out of the water, he saw heaven being torn open and the Spirit descending on him like a dove. 11 And a voice came from heaven: "You are my Son, whom I love; with you I am well pleased."

MARK 1:12-13

12 At once the Spirit sent him out into the wilderness, 13 and he was in the wilderness forty days, being tempted by Satan. He was with the wild animals, and angels attended him.

MARK 1:14b-15

[14]…Jesus went into Galilee, proclaiming the good news of God. [15] "The time has come," he said. "The kingdom of God has come near. Repent and believe the good news!"

WHAT DOES THIS MEAN FOR *US?*

The phrase "good news" originates from the Greek word *evangelion.* The English word is "gospel." Whenever Jesus preaches "the gospel," it's always connected to the good news of the arrival of His Kingdom. It means, through Him, the rule and reign of God has finally come.

What the world has been waiting for—what all those ancient tribes were looking for—is now available through Him.

He is the Messiah, the long-awaited King, the Savior who has come to rescue us. He is the guarantee that God is on His throne, He sees us, He loves us, and He keeps His promises. He can be trusted when everything else in our world is shaking.

But Jesus also uses a word that is commonly misunderstood as cold, harsh, and religious. Jesus says "repent." The word simply means to change your mind. It is a military term.

There are always two parts to repentance—you repent *from* where you were going, and you repent *to* a new direction.

When Jesus is using it here, what He's really saying is, "Which kingdom are you a part of? Where is your tribe looking for help? Whatever you have been looking for, this is your moment to come to God. Through Me, He has come to you."

This is good news because Jesus is not ignoring the problem. He knew their world was shaking. They had problems with the Roman Empire. They had challenges with the Jewish rulers. They did not feel safe. They were uncertain about the safety and the future of their families.

Jesus started His entire ministry

> **"**
> The Kingdom of God means the rule and reign of God has finally come to earth through Jesus.

project by saying "the time has come, God is here, and you can be included in this new Kingdom if you repent and believe."

You can't earn it. You don't work your way into it. You receive it through Him.

Matthew's account tells us this is what Jesus did. He taught this message in the synagogue (where the community went to worship and talk about God), He proclaimed the good news of the Kingdom, and He healed every disease and sickness among the people.

To us, this sounds like two different things. But not to them. It was not teaching and miracles. It all related to the "good news" Jesus came to bring. He demonstrated God was with them by healing the sick. These were more than spiritual ideas. His Kingdom had come.

Over 2,000 years later, Jesus has not changed His message.

EPHESIANS 2:8-9
8 For it is by grace you have been saved, through faith—and this is not from yourselves, it is the gift of God— 9 not by works, so that no one can boast.

MATTHEW 4:23
Jesus went throughout Galilee, teaching in their synagogues, proclaiming the good news of the kingdom, and healing every disease and sickness among the people.

WHAT DO I DO WITH THIS?

What did you think the message of Jesus was?

If we're not careful, we can think of Jesus as the founder of a religion instead of a King who has come to save us.

We can easily slip into the notion of trying to do good spiritual things to earn help from God. The problem is, this leaves us worn-out, exhausted, frustrated with others who are not doing what we do, and unsure of where we stand with God.

When you feel like your world is shaking, where do you look for help?
- **Do you look to your career?**
- **Your financial security?**
- **The economy?**
- **The comfort of your family and your relationships?**

In and of themselves, none of these things are bad. But they are incomplete. They are gifts from God, but they cannot do for us what only He can do.

When we put a strain on them they were never meant to endure, it becomes clear that they cannot stand up to the inevitable shaking that comes in our lives.

The good news of the Kingdom is that there is One who can never be shaken. None of us like the shaking we endure. We do not look forward to it. But when it comes, we need to let it point us to the One who is still on His throne. The One who has brought His Kingdom, His rule and reign, and made it available to us.

PSALM 62:1-2

[1] Truly my soul finds rest in God; my salvation comes from him.
[2] Truly he is my rock and my salvation; he is my fortress, I will never be shaken.

SUMMARY

INTRO WEEK 1

It's easy to feel like everything around us is shaking, and oftentimes it is. Jesus brought God's Kingdom to earth to bring back the rule and reign of God to rescue us from our shaking world.

WHY IS IT SO EASY TO *MISS THE KINGDOM OF GOD?*

PASSAGE:
MATTHEW 13:31-33

MEMORY VERSE:
PSALM 103:19

PAGES 15-28

CONCEPT

Imagine if everything in your life was exactly how God intended it to be. Is that something you would be interested in? Would you be excited to experience it for yourself?

This is what the people heard when Jesus said, "The Kingdom of God has come near."

The Kingdom of God is one of the big themes that run all the way through the Bible.

Jesus talked about the Kingdom more than anything else.

When He preached the "good news" (the gospel), He always talked about the Kingdom.

When He sent His disciples out to preach, He told them to talk about the Kingdom.

So why do so many people miss it?

Because the Kingdom doesn't work the way we expect. It doesn't work like other kingdoms. It doesn't come through an army or earthly, political structures.

Remember, when Jesus talks about the Kingdom of God, He's not talking about a castle or a palace. He's not talking about a specific nation. He is saying that the Kingdom is wherever God is ruling and reigning. That is what He came to do.

This concept goes all the way back to the very first chapter of the Bible. When God made man and woman in His image in Genesis chapter one, He intended for them to rule over all the creatures in the sea and on the land. He invited the first people to partner with Him in caring for His creation, which He called "very good."

Everything was perfect. It was "paradise." It was exactly how God intended—until man disobeyed God, betrayed His trust, rejected God's Kingdom in pursuit of their own, and as a result, sin entered the world.

Sin fundamentally altered the nature of man and fractured the image of God. It was still in there, but it was harder to see. Work became difficult and unfulfilling. Relationships became dysfunctional. The perfect paradise had been shaken.

God wasn't surprised by this. He knew where this story would go before it began. He had a plan to restore His Kingdom through a perfect King. But not until the proper time.

The descendants of these first people spread out over the earth. In their brokenness, they tried to build their own kingdoms to reclaim the paradise they were created for. We are still trying—this is the human story.

The Old Testament follows the story as these groups of people formed tribes and built cultures. God continued to work with people who trusted Him, and He made a

GENESIS 1:26
Then God said, "Let us make mankind in our image, in our likeness, so that they may rule over the fish in the sea and the birds in the sky, over the livestock and all the wild animals, and over all the creatures that move along the ground."

GENESIS 1:31
God saw all that he had made, and it was very good. And there was evening, and there was morning—the sixth day.

You can find this story in Genesis 3. It sets up the rest of the Bible.

covenant with a man named Abraham. God promised to make a special people out of this family, and He kept His word.

Abraham's great-grandson Joseph was betrayed by his brothers and ended up in Egypt. God was with this young man, who served the king of Egypt, the biggest kingdom in the world, and through him, the whole world was saved.

This family was blessed in Egypt until they numbered in the millions. The king of Egypt began to fear them, so he treated them terribly, but God supernaturally rescued His people from Egypt and their powerful king.

God's plan was to bring them into a Promised Land where He would rule and reign with them. But once again the people struggled to trust Him and instead wanted to do things their own way. What should have taken days ended up taking decades, and when the people finally entered the land, they looked around and realized the other nations had kings.

They decided they wanted one too. They wanted to be like everyone else. They still believed their better option was building their own kingdom instead of receiving the one God had for them.

God knew where this road would lead—pain and suffering. But He honored their choice. He gave them a king. And outside of a few bright spots, for the next several thousand years, God's people are repeatedly disappointed by the failures of human kingdoms.

Their own kings led them astray and let them down. Other kingdoms—the Assyrians, the Babylonians, the Persians, the Greeks, and eventually the Romans—ruled and reigned over them.

They knew what it was like to try all these other kingdoms. None of them delivered on the promise.

So when Jesus shows up and says God's Kingdom has finally come through Him, He is saying that thousands of years of global history have led to this moment.

It's kind of a big deal.

This is what makes our theme verse for the series so meaningful (Hebrews 12:28):

> **Therefore, since we are receiving a kingdom that cannot be shaken, let us be thankful, and so worship God acceptably with reverence and awe…**

Because of King Jesus, this Kingdom cannot be shaken. Unlike every other kingdom, this one will never be overthrown or fade away.

PASSAGE

IN CONTEXT

In the Gospel of Matthew, Jesus talks more about the Kingdom than any other book in the Bible. Most of the time, Matthew uses the phrase "kingdom of heaven" instead of "kingdom of God." But he is not confused and he's not talking about heaven the way we typically think of it.

Because he is writing to a primarily Jewish audience, Matthew is using what scholars call a "circumlocution." It is a roundabout way of speaking, or a euphemism. According to tradition, God's name was holy, so out of their reverence to Him, they didn't use it casually.

The God of the Bible is not one of these rival tribal gods. He is not the God of one group of people—He is God over *all* people. He is the one true God. He is the ruler of heaven and earth. He does not sit on a throne made by human hands.

Matthew uses this phrase "kingdom of heaven" to reinforce and affirm this high view of God.

Another striking detail of the way Jesus talks about the Kingdom in Matthew is the constant mystery

MATTHEW 4:17

From that time on Jesus began to preach, "Repent, for the kingdom of heaven has come near."

and secrecy He uses. Jesus consistently teaches through parables—short stories intended to intrigue the listener into processing through the various layers of meaning.

The crowd and the disciples would consistently find themselves confused. Jesus was okay with this. His primary goal was not the exchange of information—it was an invitation into an ongoing relationship.

His goal has not changed.

In Matthew chapter 13, Jesus gives seven different parables to describe what the "kingdom of heaven" is like. He takes the time to unpack and explain two of the longer parables for His disciples (the sower and the weeds), but the other five He leaves up in the air.

He wants us to ask questions and consider what this means for us.

Read Matthew 13:31-33 on page 22. $\Longrightarrow$

MATTHEW 13:31-33

[31] He told them another parable: "The kingdom of heaven is like a mustard seed, which a man took and planted in his field. [32] Though it is the smallest of all seeds, yet when it grows, it is the largest of garden plants and becomes a tree, so that the birds come and perch in its branches." [33] He told them still another parable: "The kingdom of heaven is like yeast that a woman took and mixed into about sixty pounds of flour until it worked all through the dough."

WHAT DOES THIS MEAN FOR *US?*

> > > Our understanding of the Kingdom starts small. The mustard seed was the smallest seed in this part of the world. It was an easy reference point. This is why Jesus points to it. But even though it's small, the potential is there for great things and a big impact. All that is required is patience and intentionality.

God is not asking us to have all the answers or all these terms and concepts memorized. He's not primarily checking for information; He's looking for interest.

If we're hungry, if we're curious, if we want to grow, He will meet us in that place. As we'll discover through this series, Jesus does not bring the Kingdom to the people who know the most and who live the best lives. He brings it to the willing, the curious, and the committed.

It's not good news for a select few; it's good news to anyone who receives it with a willing heart.

If we're preoccupied, if we're distracted, if we're more interested in other things, or if we give ourselves to a different kingdom, we will miss out on what God has for us.

This is how God works with us and in us. It starts small, but over time, the impact becomes great.

The same is true for yeast. Yeast is small and therefore can appear insignificant. The fact that we can't see it doesn't mean it's not working. It doesn't wait for us to understand in order to be effective.

Sixty pounds is a lot of flour. How long would it take for the yeast to work its way through that much dough? A long time. It requires patience. The same is true for the Kingdom. But think about how great the impact will be. How many loaves of bread could you make with that much dough?

Far too many people have the perspective that a relationship with God can be segmented off to the occasional religious service—that somehow our spirituality stays confined in a separate compartment without much influence on our daily lives.

Jesus is directly confronting this view. This is not how His Kingdom works.

Like the yeast working its way through the dough, the message of the Kingdom touches every area of our lives. It impacts the way we think, we feel, we see ourselves, the way we view and relate to God, and the way we love and serve others.

There is no part of our lives the Kingdom cannot transform.

In Luke 17, the Pharisees are questioning Jesus for more details on when His Kingdom would come. Jesus challenges their view. They don't get it. He tells them it's already in their midst. Like yeast, it works from the inside out.

Not only does Jesus' metaphor apply to our personal lives, it applies to the whole world. The message of the Kingdom of God started small, but over the past 2,000 years it has moved through time, language, culture, country, and history....all the way to you.

LUKE 17:20-21
[20] *Once, on being asked by the Pharisees when the kingdom of God would come, Jesus replied, "The coming of the kingdom of God is not something that can be observed, [21] nor will people say, 'Here it is,' or 'There it is,' because the kingdom of God is in your midst."*

WHAT DO I DO WITH THIS?

The goal isn't to have all the right information about the Kingdom. The disciples were consistently confused and routinely made mistakes.

But they were committed to Jesus and His Kingdom, and because of this, when we look back over their lives, we can easily see the impact of the Kingdom changing them from the inside out.

Which kingdom is easier to see growing in your life: the Kingdom of God or your own kingdom?

Have you tried to segment your spirituality or your relationship with God to one portion of your life, or is it impacting everything?

Can you see clear evidence of the rule and reign of God in your life? Can anyone else see it?

PSALM 103:19

The Lord has established his throne in heaven, and his kingdom rules over all.

SUMMARY

INTRO WEEK 2

Jesus promises to bring His Kingdom to those who receive Him. The way we experience His unshakable Kingdom is to receive it in exchange for the fragile kingdom we are building.

WHY *DOES IT MATTER* IF GOD IS STILL ON HIS *THRONE?*

PASSAGE:
LUKE 11:1-2

MEMORY VERSE:
PSALM 47:8

PAGES 29-44

CONCEPT

There is an old saying followers of Christ have used to bring comfort in uncertain times: "Well… God is still on His throne."

This is a biblical idea. Psalm 47:8 says, "God reigns over the nations; God is seated on his holy throne."

Why does this help us? Why does it matter? Because so often in life, things don't make sense.

- **We're blindsided by relational challenges in our family.**
- **The deal at work we've dedicated a year to falls apart.**
- **Someone we love is in a terrible accident.**

When everything around us feels like it's shaking, we reach for something that won't fall apart. God meets us in those moments. More than simple solutions, He offers us Himself.

We can find confidence not in our ability to understand what God is doing but in the fact that He is in control. And this confidence gives us the ability to overcome all of the shaking we experience in our lives.

This is what it means to be included in His Kingdom. It does not mean we no longer have problems or pain, but in every situation we are given the confidence that we are known and loved by the One who is in control.

To say that God is still on His throne is to say that God is in control. And He is. At all times.

We live in an anxious world. It has always been a challenge for human beings, but it has become our dominant issue in recent years. It is the single leading cause of our collective lack of mental health.

Anxiety is the body's response to worry and fear. It starts as an emotion and then it takes a physical toll on our bodies.

A common cause of anxiety in our culture today is technology. It gives us constant access to everything that is happening at all times. Human beings have never been exposed to this much information. Because it spreads more quickly and stays with us longer, negative information is prioritized across all our channels because it allows them to monetize our information.

We were created to manage a few specific threats we face on a daily basis. We were not designed to manage all the potential threats that might develop anywhere in the world.

We were not designed to manage all the potential threats that might develop anywhere in the world.

One of the most damaging things about anxiety is the amount of time we spend worried and afraid about things that haven't even happened yet. All it takes is the possibility that something could happen, and we begin

to "catastrophize" by imagining the worst-case scenario. This is a common response because we think that by preparing ourselves, we will somehow lessen the pain we might experience.

Unfortunately, this strategy almost always backfires. It doesn't reduce the amount of pain and worry we experience; it multiplies it.

Jesus offers us a better way.

He faced unimaginable challenges and problems. He experienced pain beyond what we understand. But He consistently found comfort in the fact that His Father was in control. No matter how much the earth was shaking—and for Jesus it literally did—God was still on His throne.

When we receive His Kingdom, when we come under His rule and reign, we can find this same comfort.

MATTHEW 27:50-51
[50] And when Jesus had cried out again in a loud voice, he gave up his spirit. [51] At that moment the curtain of the temple was torn in two from top to bottom. The earth shook, the rocks split...

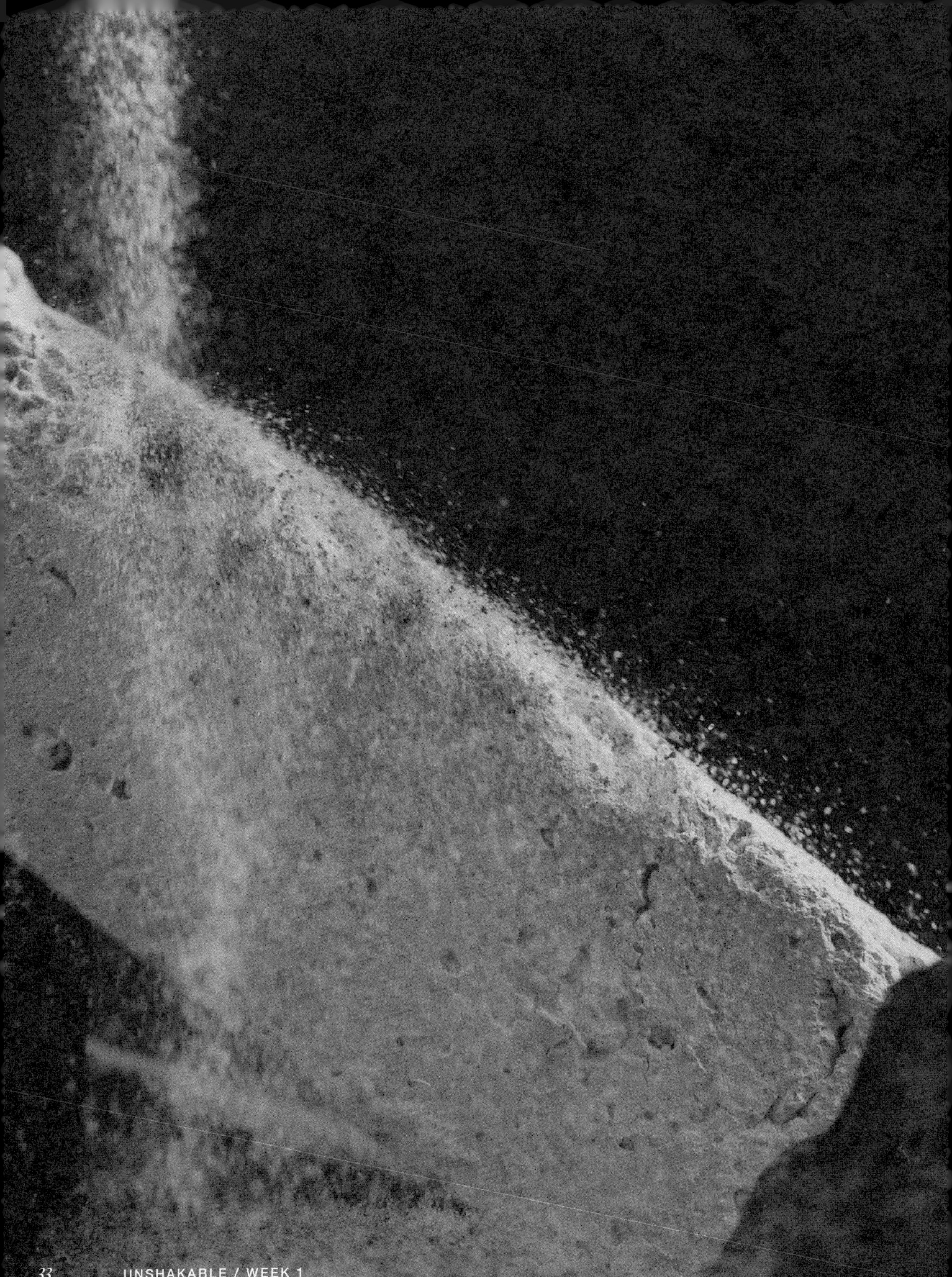

PASSAGE

IN CONTEXT

Jesus and His disciples have been ministering in their region. They're preaching the good news of the Kingdom of God, praying for the sick, and performing miracles. The crowds of people following them are growing.

When they first started following Jesus, they must have wondered what was going to happen or if they had made a mistake. Now, people are responding and huge crowds are following Him.

In Luke's Gospel, the disciples quickly realized how regularly Jesus would withdraw from the crowds of people to pray. They recognized a pattern. When crowds, pressure, and general worries increased, Jesus would go off and pray.

Remember, for Jesus prayer was not a religious obligation. It may be hard for us to understand, but He had been with the Father for all eternity. When He went to pray, He was distancing Himself from the problems and attitudes of the world. He was reconnecting with His Father and, in His humanity, was experiencing the rule and reign of God.

LUKE 5:16 ◀◆▶
But Jesus often withdrew to lonely places and prayed.

By the time we get to Luke 11, the disciples have figured out this connection. Jesus has a strength, a confidence, and an ability to face challenges they don't have. They realize something happens when He prays. Somehow He has an assurance that no matter what happens, God is in control. They want in on this.

They realize one of the ways this happens is through prayer.

Read Luke 11:1-2 on page 36. ⟶

Prayer is not an opportunity to show off how spiritual you are to others. Prayer is more than a list of complaints—even though God wants us to tell Him what we're worried about. First and foremost, prayer is relational. It connects us with God. We bring everything to Him—our emotions, our worries, our fears, and our hearts.

◀▶ **Prayer is relational.**

The disciples ask Jesus to teach them how to pray. He starts with acknowledging the holiness of God. The word "hallowed" means "sanctified," or "to make holy." To say God is "holy" is to say He is other. He's not like us; He is higher, He is uncreated, He is unique.

He sits on His throne all by Himself. Jesus wanted us to know all prayer starts with this idea, as well as our understanding of God's Kingdom.

Why would He connect prayer with His Kingdom? Because the Kingdom is not a place or a structure; it's the rule and reign of God. When the Kingdom comes, everything lines up with how God intends it to be.

Matthew's version of this story includes "...your kingdom come, your will be done, on earth as it is in heaven." This emphasizes heaven as the place where God's reign is perfect, and so when we pray that the Kingdom would come on earth, we're asking Him to close the gap between the two.

◀ ▶ **MATTHEW 6:9-10**
9 "This, then, is how you should pray:
'Our Father in heaven, hallowed be your name,
10 your kingdom come, your will be done, on earth as it is in heaven.'"

LUKE 11:1-2

[1] One day Jesus was praying in a certain place. When he finished, one of his disciples said to him, "Lord, teach us to pray, just as John taught his disciples."
[2] He said to them, "When you pray, say: 'Father, hallowed be your name, your kingdom come.'"

WHAT DOES THIS MEAN FOR *US?*

Jesus showed us how to find strength in the fact that God is on His throne.

The goal is not to live free from anxiety or fear. Those emotions are part of life. But we don't have to be a prisoner to them. We are not helpless when our lives start shaking.

We do not know what tomorrow is going to bring. And even if we did, this information may give us advance warning, but that's not the same as having the confidence to hold on to that which cannot be shaken.

This starts with a relational connection to God. When things are shaking, we move toward Him, not away from Him.

Jesus also showed us how prayer can help. It connects our hearts, our worries, our emotions, and our anxieties with the person and the power of God. He is never surprised by what we are going through. Our latest challenge, no matter how much it may worry us, cannot knock Him off His throne.

This is not one of those moments when Jesus hides the answer in a secret parable. He makes it simple. When you're worried, when you're afraid, get close to your Father and pray. Don't move away from Him; move toward Him.

To comfort us, our culture has taken to the phrase "Everything happens for a reason." This is not what Jesus is saying.

In our uncertainty, we hold on to God, His Word, and His presence. Even when it seems like everything is falling apart, He can be trusted. We don't throw away our confidence—it has a great reward.

Remember, Jesus told us to pray that His Kingdom would come on earth as it is in heaven. When we hold on to our confidence and pray, when we turn our hearts and our minds toward Him, we can experience today what we will experience every day when we are with Him in heaven.

> **HEBREWS 10:35-36**
> [35] So do not throw away your confidence; it will be richly rewarded. [36] You need to persevere so that when you have done the will of God, you will receive what he has promised.

WHAT DO I DO WITH THIS?

Do you know how to find comfort in the fact God is in control? Does it produce confidence in you?

How do you respond when you're feeling anxious? Is it your tendency to get more information and to try and come up with your own solutions?

Does your mind race to the worst-case scenario and catastrophize in order to prepare yourself for any and all outcomes?

The next time you feel anxious or afraid, remember the example of Jesus. Remember the lifestyle He modeled for the disciples. He withdrew to be with His Father and to pray. He needed to know God was still on His throne. If Jesus needed this, how much more could we benefit from adopting this simple process?

PSALM 47:8

God reigns over the nations; God is seated on his holy throne.

DISCUSSION

1.
How big is the issue of anxiety in our culture? In what ways do you see anxiety affecting people?

2.
What are some common causes of anxiety?

3.
How do you typically respond when you feel anxious? What do you do? (Include both negative and positive responses.)

4.
How does prayer help when we're feeling anxious?

5. Do you believe God is in control, no matter what? How does your belief about this question affect you?

6. Read Matthew 6:9-10. Why should prayer begin by focusing on God's holiness?

7. Read Matthew 6:9-10 again. What does it mean to pray for God's Kingdom to come? Why should we pray this prayer?

8. How does knowing that God is on His throne give us confidence in every situation?

APPLICATION

Is there anything you're anxious about right now? If so, what is it? Spend a few minutes talking to God about it. What can you do to place your confidence in God?

SUMMARY

WEEK ONE

When we trust in our own strength, it leaves us anxious and worried. But God's Kingdom brings us security and stability. We can confidently place our trust in the unshakable throne of Jesus and connect with our King in prayer.

WHY DON'T MORE PEOPLE *EXPERIENCE* THE KINGDOM OF GOD?

PASSAGE:
JOHN 3:1-18

MEMORY VERSE:
1 PETER 1:8

PAGES 45-60

CONCEPT

The only thing worse than feeling like your life is falling apart is not being able to see why it's happening or where it's coming from.

Have you ever been on an airplane in a storm? You can hear the pilots preparing you for what is coming. You can see the flight attendants moving quickly through the cabin. They want you to secure your things, put your tables up, and fasten your seatbelt, because things are about to start shaking.

But you can't see the turbulence or what's happening outside.

If you're the kind of person who likes a little adventure, you probably enjoy theme parks and roller coasters. When the ride takes off, you feel it in your gut. But if the ride is in the dark, you have no idea which way it's going to turn. This only increases the adrenaline because you can't see what will happen next.

At times, life feels the same way. We often feel most vulnerable when we don't see the shaking coming.

- **We didn't feel great, but it didn't seem like a big deal until the medical reports came back. Now everything feels like it's falling apart.**

- **We knew things in our marriage were a little bumpy, but we couldn't see how bad it really was.**

- **Work had been a struggle the last few weeks, but we had no way of predicting how difficult it was about to get.**

Each of these challenges is unique, but they produce the same result: our whole world is shaking.

This also explains why it can be so difficult for us to find comfort in the fact that God is in control and He is still on His throne. We may trust this is true, but it's hard when we can't see Him.

Jesus appreciates this difficulty. He knows how hard it is to trust something you can't see. That's why He spent so much time preaching about a Kingdom that had come because He knew most people could not see it.

They didn't know where to look, and even if they did, they couldn't see it.

PASSAGE

IN CONTEXT

In the Gospel of John, Jesus only uses the word "kingdom" three times, but two of them come from one of the most well-known passages of the entire Bible. This does not mean John fails to capture Jesus' focus on the Kingdom, but he approaches it from a different angle. While the other Gospels weave the Kingdom through parables and mystery, John jumps right into explaining the significance of what Jesus is saying.

Early in Jesus' ministry, a Pharisee named Nicodemus asks to meet with Him at night. Most scholars believe this detail is included to imply Nicodemus was reluctant to be seen with Jesus because He was already controversial and unpopular with the Pharisees.

Jesus would use this nighttime encounter to teach Nicodemus an important lesson about the Kingdom of God.

Read John 3:1-18 on page 49-50.

JOHN 3:1-18

[1] Now there was a Pharisee, a man named Nicodemus who was a member of the Jewish ruling council. [2] He came to Jesus at night and said, "Rabbi, we know that you are a teacher who has come from God. For no one could perform the signs you are doing if God were not with him."

[3] Jesus replied, "Very truly I tell you, no one can see the kingdom of God unless they are born again."

[4] "How can someone be born when they are old?" Nicodemus asked. "Surely they cannot enter a second time into their mother's womb to be born!"

[5] Jesus answered, "Very truly I tell you, no one can enter the kingdom of God unless they are born of water and the Spirit. [6] Flesh gives birth to flesh, but the Spirit gives birth to spirit. [7] You should not be surprised at my saying, 'You must be born again.' [8] The wind blows wherever it pleases. You hear its sound, but you cannot tell where it comes from or

where it is going. So it is with everyone born of the Spirit." 9 "How can this be?" Nicodemus asked.

10 "You are Israel's teacher," said Jesus, "and do you not understand these things? 11 Very truly I tell you, we speak of what we know, and we testify to what we have seen, but still you people do not accept our testimony. 12 I have spoken to you of earthly things and you do not believe; how then will you believe if I speak of heavenly things? 13 No one has ever gone into heaven except the one who came from heaven — the Son of Man. 14 Just as Moses lifted up the snake in the wilderness, so the Son of Man must be lifted up, 15 that everyone who believes may have eternal life in him."

16 For God so loved the world that he gave his one and only Son, that whoever believes in him shall not perish but have eternal life. 17 For God did not send his Son into the world to condemn the world, but to save the world through him. 18 Whoever believes in him is not condemned, but whoever does not believe stands condemned already because they have not believed in the name of God's one and only Son.

The Pharisee Nicodemus is certainly intrigued by Jesus. The fact that Jesus did more than teach—He also performed miracles—was an endorsement to Nicodemus that Jesus had come from God.

Jesus can feel the internal struggle Nicodemus is wrestling through. This man senses the presence of God. He recognizes something special is happening in and through this man, Jesus, but it doesn't fit any of the spiritual or religious categories Nicodemus has encountered.

Jesus won't fit neatly in his box.

Jesus explains why this is hard for Nicodemus. He tells him that no one can see the Kingdom of God—we can't understand it; we can't get our arms around it—until we're born again. This doesn't make things any clearer for Nicodemus. In the ancient world, the person who knew the most spiritual information, and who understood religious intricacies, was the mature one.

Jesus shakes Nicodemus' whole approach. According to Jesus, it's not what you know but whether or not you simply trust and believe that brings you close to God. He tells him the only way to enter the Kingdom is to be born of water and the Spirit. Jesus tells Nicodemus none of this should be surprising to someone who understands the things of God.

Now he's really confused.

At this point, Jesus lovingly teases this spiritual leader. He tells Nicodemus if he's the one teaching all of God's people, he should probably understand the basics of how a relationship with God works. It's not about what we know but what we believe.

This is when Jesus tells Nicodemus the most famous verse in the Bible—the verse most children memorize first: God

JOHN 3:16
For God so loved the world that he gave his one and only Son, that whoever believes in him shall not perish but have eternal life.

JOHN 7:45-52
45 Finally the temple guards went back to the chief priests and the Pharisees, who asked them, "Why didn't you bring him in?" 46 "No one ever spoke the way this man does," the guards replied. 47 "You mean he has deceived you also?" the Pharisees retorted. 48 "Have any of the rulers or of the Pharisees believed in him? 49 No! But this mob that knows nothing of the law—there is a curse on them."
50 Nicodemus, who had gone to Jesus earlier and who was one of their own number, asked, 51 "Does our law condemn a man without first hearing him to find out what he has been doing?"
52 They replied, "Are you from Galilee, too? Look into it, and you will find that a prophet does not come out of Galilee."

loved the world so much that He gave His only Son. He didn't send His Son to condemn the world but to love and save it. Unfortunately, most people choose darkness over light.

JOHN 19:38-42
38 Later, Joseph of Arimathea asked Pilate for the body of Jesus. Now Joseph was a disciple of Jesus, but secretly because he feared the Jewish leaders. With Pilate's permission, he came and took the body away. 39 He was accompanied by Nicodemus, the man who earlier had visited Jesus at night. Nicodemus brought a mixture of myrrh and aloes, about seventy-five pounds. 40 Taking Jesus' body, the two of them wrapped it, with the spices, in strips of linen. This was in accordance with Jewish burial customs. 41 At the place where Jesus was crucified, there was a garden, and in the garden a new tomb, in which no one had ever been laid. 42 Because it was the Jewish day of Preparation and since the tomb was nearby, they laid Jesus there.

One of the most interesting things about this famous interaction is that Nicodemus does not see the Kingdom yet. We have no reason to believe he received Jesus and was born again at that moment.

But he didn't disappear either. Jesus did not give him an ultimatum that night. He did not say, "It's now or never!" He gave Nicodemus space to keep searching.

In John 7, the Pharisees are upset with the temple guards for failing to arrest Jesus. They're looking for a reason to throw Him in jail. But Nicodemus steps up to defend Jesus.

Clearly, Jesus was having an impact on this man.

By the time we get to John 19, the guards and Pharisees have accomplished their goal. Jesus was crucified, and when they pulled His body down, some of His "secret disciples" went to the Roman governor Pilate and asked for His body. They were secret because they were afraid of the Jewish leaders. They had brought 75 pounds of burial spices to prepare Him to be wrapped and laid in the tomb. The first was a man named Joseph of Arimathea.

The other was Nicodemus.

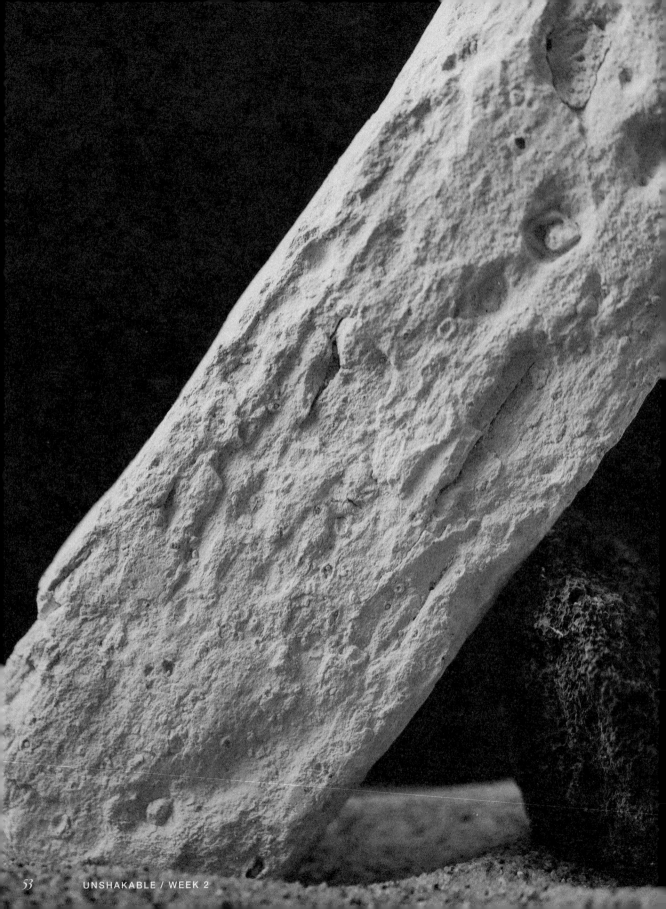

WHAT DOES THIS MEAN FOR *US?*

Most people equate seeing with believing. They think, *If I could see it for myself, I would believe.* Jesus explains that the Kingdom does not work this way.

You won't see it until you believe.

Spiritual depth or religious maturity does not come from facts we know—it comes from how deeply we believe what we know to be true. Does it impact the way we think? The way we talk? The way we live? This is how the Kingdom works.

Jesus is okay with our process. He's patient with us. He invites our questions and our challenges. But He doesn't always offer answers—He offers Himself.

This is what happened to Nicodemus. We don't know all the details. We don't know what changed. But we know

something did. Because he went from being scared to being known as a friend of Jesus, to standing before the Roman governor after they killed Him for claiming to be the King.

No one likes it when life starts shaking. And it's especially difficult when we can't see why it's happening or where it's coming from.

But when everything around us is shaking, we reach for something that can't be shaken. Jesus does not offer us solutions to all our problems. He offers us Himself. He gives us His Kingdom. He gives us His peace. We don't get to dictate our terms. We either receive Him or we don't.

Later in his life, Jesus' disciple and close friend Peter is writing to a group of Christians who are going through incredibly difficult challenges. Some of them have been

killed because of their faith in Jesus. He is encouraging them to hold on.

He tells them, "Though you have not seen him, you love him; and even though you do not see him now, you believe in him and are filled with an inexpressible and glorious joy..." (1 Peter 1:8)

We like to sing song lyrics like,

"Even when *
I don't
see
it,
You're
working,"

because we know God is always up to more than what we can see with our eyes.

If we decide to trust only what we see, we end up missing out on so much of what God wants to do in us and for us.

* These lyrics are from the song "Way Maker," originally written by Nigerian gospel singer/ songwriter Sinach.

WHAT DO I DO WITH THIS?

Are you waiting for more information or more answers in order to trust Jesus?

Are you hoping to see more so you can make a more informed decision?

Do you believe God loved the world so much He sent His only Son so that whoever believes in Him will not perish but have eternal life?

This is more than the most famous verse—it can become real for you.

What's holding you back?

If you have received Him, today is a great day to remember the blessing of trusting that God is working and moving even when we can't see Him. His goodness and His Kingdom extend far beyond what we can see.

When we put our trust in this,
He fills us with inexpressible joy.
That's worth holding on to.

1 PETER 1:8

Though you have not
seen him, you love him;
and even though you
do not see him now, you
believe in him and are
filled with an inexpressible
and glorious joy...

DISCUSSION

1. Read John 3:1-2. What draws Nicodemus to Jesus?

2. In verse 3, Jesus tells Nicodemus that "no one can see the Kingdom of God unless they are born again." What do you think it means to be born again?

3. Why can't we see God's Kingdom until we believe?

4. Sometimes we think spiritual maturity is about knowing facts. But where does Jesus say spiritual maturity comes from?

5. How can our "understanding" sometimes get in the way of seeing Jesus for who He is?

6. In John 3, Nicodemus is clearly intrigued by Jesus, but he doesn't know what to make of Him yet. Where are you at in your relationship with Jesus? Are you (a) uncertain and skeptical, (b) intrigued and seeking answers, or (c) bought in and born again? Explain.

7. Think about the story of Nicodemus throughout the book of John. How could his story parallel yours? Explain.

8. Read 1 Peter 1:8. According to this verse, what does God fill us with when we believe in Him? How have you experienced this in your life?

APPLICATION

Have you believed in Jesus and fully surrendered your life to Him? If not, you can right now. All you have to do is believe and say this simple prayer:

···

Jesus,
I believe You are the Son of God.
I believe You died on the cross
for my sins and that You rose again.
I believe You love me and want to
reveal Yourself to me. Please forgive
me of my sins and become my
Savior and Lord. I want to know
You and see Your Kingdom.
In Jesus' name I pray. Amen.

···

If you said that prayer, *congratulations—you are now born again!* This is the start of an amazing new journey!

Please let your Small Group know that you prayed this prayer today. They will want to celebrate with you and help you grow in your new relationship with God.

SUMMARY

WEEK TWO

To receive God's Kingdom, we first have to see it. There is one clear step to receiving the Kingdom of God—accepting eternal life available only through the King. The Kingdom, and all its glory, comes to those who receive Jesus by faith.

WHAT *DOES* THE KINGDOM OF GOD *PRODUCE* IN US?

PASSAGE:
ROMANS 14:17-18

MEMORY VERSE:
1 CORINTHIANS 4:20

PAGES 61-74

CONCEPT

There are lots of reasons why it's not easy for us to relate to this notion of the Kingdom.

Our culture tells us every day, in all kinds of ways, to put ourselves first. Nothing is more important than our personal happiness, being "true" to ourselves, pursuing what we deserve, and even "living our truth." Human nature loves all of these messages because selfishness comes naturally to us.

This could not be more opposite to the biblical message of the Kingdom.

We are not the King. We are not the center of the Kingdom.

On the contrary, we are received and welcomed into the Kingdom through the grace and love of the King, not on the basis of what we have earned or deserve.

It only takes a few moments working with children to realize how deeply ingrained this is in each of us. Without any effort or intention, our default setting is "What's in it for me?" Deep down, we're all consumers looking for how we can get the most of what we want for the lowest price.

The problem is, this Kingdom doesn't work with a consumer mindset.

We like the benefits of being a consumer, but we don't like the culture it produces. When everyone puts their own needs first, relationships quickly become transactional. We end up exploiting each other. Trust disappears.

When Jesus talked about the culture of His Kingdom, He said the greatest of all was the servant. He said the last would be first. He said those who try to save their lives would lose it, but those who lose their lives for His sake will find them in Him.

He said the distracted and the proud who turned down the invitation would be left out, while the ones no one expected would be welcomed in.

The Kingdom Jesus came to bring is not primarily about religious information and spiritual knowledge. When it comes, it's always more than words. It changes the environment.

We all want the benefits of what the Kingdom produces, but they don't come the way we expect and we don't get to pick and choose how we receive them.

First and foremost, the Kingdom is not about us. We are invited into the Kingdom by a King, who came as a servant and calls us to serve and love others the way He does.

When we try to make it about us, eventually things in our life will begin to shake. It's only when we build on His Kingdom that we can trust, no matter what happens, He's still on His throne.

MATTHEW 23:11
The greatest among you will be your servant.

MATTHEW 20:16
So the last will be first, and the first will be last.

MATTHEW 10:39-40
39 Whoever finds their life will lose it, and whoever loses their life for my sake will find it. 40 Anyone who welcomes you welcomes me, and anyone who welcomes me welcomes the one who sent me.

PASSAGE

IN CONTEXT

ACTS 19:8

Paul entered the synagogue and spoke boldly there for three months, arguing persuasively about the kingdom of God.

ACTS 20:25

Now I know that none of you among whom I have gone about preaching the kingdom will ever see me again.

ACTS 28:23

They arranged to meet Paul on a certain day, and came in even larger numbers to the place where he was staying. He witnessed to them from morning till evening, explaining about the kingdom of God, and from the Law of Moses and from the Prophets he tried to persuade them about Jesus.

ACTS 28:31

He proclaimed the kingdom of God and taught about the Lord Jesus Christ—with all boldness and without hindrance!

The apostle Paul was one of the most significant leaders in the early church. Before he met Jesus himself, he persecuted and resisted the church and followers of Jesus. After meeting Jesus on the road to Damascus, Paul's life was completely transformed. He spent the rest of his years preaching the gospel of the Kingdom of God.

Multiple places in the book of Acts tell us Paul would spend months persuasively communicating, preaching, explaining, and proclaiming the message of the Kingdom of God.

He planted churches throughout the ancient world and wrote almost a third of the New Testament. His longest and most exhaustive letter, Romans, was written to a large group of believers in the capital city of Rome. Multiple times he tried to make the trip to visit them, but most scholars believe he never made it to them.

Toward the end of the letter, Paul is coaching these new followers of Christ how to practically serve and love one another. Some of them wanted to eat meat; some only ate vegetables. Some of them thought one day was more sacred than another. These preferences were growing into strong opinions and reasons for people to look down on each other and pass judgment.

These opinions and judgments were creating relational challenges among the believers, and Paul wanted it to stop. This group of believers had lost sight of the fact that Jesus told His disciples the world would know they loved Him because of the way they loved each other.

Read Romans 14:17-18 on page 66.

The culture of the Kingdom is not the freedom to do whatever you feel like, no matter what anyone else says. This is the attitude of the world. In the Kingdom, our freedom gives us the ability to think of the other person and to love and serve them.

When we turn our personal preferences into demands for how our brothers and sisters live, we've lost the culture of the Kingdom. But when we set aside our preferences in order to love and serve others, we help make the Kingdom real in a way others can receive it.

JOHN 17:20-23

[20]*My prayer is not for them alone. I pray also for those who will believe in me through their message,* [21] *that all of them may be one, Father, just as you are in me and I am in you. May they also be in us so that the world may believe that you have sent me.* [22] *I have given them the glory that you gave me, that they may be one as we are one—* [23] *I in them and you in me—so that they may be brought to complete unity. Then the world will know that you sent me and have loved them even as you have loved me.*

ROMANS 14:17-18

[17] For the kingdom of God is not a matter of eating and drinking, but of righteousness, peace and joy in the Holy Spirit, [18] because anyone who serves Christ in this way is pleasing to God and receives human approval.

WHAT DOES THIS MEAN FOR *US?*

> > > When we try to set ourselves up as the center of our lives, we end up disappointed.

You know that difficult person in your life? The one who always finds something to complain about? No matter how thoughtful, how loving, and how caring they're treated, they always have a comment.

This is about that. Don't be that person. This is not how the Kingdom works.

Remember, God's Kingdom is the rule and reign of God. It means things are flowing the way He intended. And when this is happening, it's always more than words.

It's more *show me* than *tell me*.

Paul is saying you can tell the Kingdom is present because you can feel the righteousness, peace, and joy in the Holy Spirit. This is what the Kingdom produces in our lives.

"Righteousness" is a legal term. It means right standing with God. It's a condition God declares over you.

It's not something we earn for eating the right stuff, not eating the bad stuff, or taking special care to observe all the sacred days. Righteousness is a gift from God we receive by faith.

If we try to earn it through our perfect obedience, it's self-righteousness. Self-righteousness is exhausting, and it always leaves us frustrated with what other people did or didn't do.

Peace is another important concept in the Bible. The Hebrew word for "peace" is *shalom*. It's a blessing. It's another way of saying, "Everything is how God wants it to be." Everything is going to be alright. God is in control. God is on His throne. It's not the absence of conflict or challenge; it's the unshakable presence of God in the midst of those things.

We all want this kind of peace. Sometimes we think we can find it on vacation, or when we get the house exactly how we want it, or if we get everything done on our to-do list, or wherever else we try to find it.

But the peace of God is different. It's stronger than all those things. We can receive it in the middle of a storm or in a moment of crisis. Jesus left us His peace. He gave it to us. Not the way the world gives it. His peace gives us the ability to not be afraid or to let our hearts be troubled.

Finally, Paul says the Kingdom produces joy in the Holy Spirit. Not joy in our circumstances. Not joy because we have nothing to be worried about or afraid of. This joy is inexpressible. It can surprise us. This joy often shows up in the midst of our sorrow.

Once again we're left with a choice: make ourselves the center and expect everyone else to do what we want. Spoiler alert: the results of this approach never satisfy.

Or we can love and serve others out of our love for our King. It's not easy, it doesn't come naturally, but it produces in us His righteousness, His peace, and His joy through the power of the Holy Spirit.

When we take this approach, it pleases God and it brings blessing and approval in our relationships.

ROMANS 3:22a
This righteousness is given through faith in Jesus Christ to all who believe.

JOHN 14:27
Peace I leave with you; my peace I give you. I do not give to you as the world gives. Do not let your hearts be troubled and do not be afraid.

ROMANS 14:17
For the kingdom of God is not a matter of eating and drinking, but of righteousness, peace and joy in the Holy Spirit...

WHAT DO I DO WITH THIS?

Have you fallen into a consumer mindset? How does it impact the quality of your life?

When was the last time you treated someone in your life as a means to an end? When was the last time someone did this to you? How did it make you feel?

Do you regularly experience the righteousness of God? Or do you struggle to find the confidence that He loves you and is pleased with you?

Are you trying to find peace on your own? Or have you prioritized the gift of the peace of Jesus He promised to give you?

When was the last time you experienced joy in the midst of sorrow? It may not make sense, but it's a gift of the Kingdom.

1 CORINTHIANS 4:20

For the kingdom of God is not a matter of talk but of power.

DISCUSSION

1. How would you describe the differences between a consumer mindset and a Kingdom mindset? Which do you gravitate toward? Explain.

2. Read Romans 3:22a. How are we made righteous?

3. Have you been trying to earn your righteousness, or do you realize you simply receive God's righteousness through faith? Explain.

4. How would you describe the biblical concept of peace (Hebrew: *shalom*)?

5. Have you experienced God's peace in your life, even through difficult circumstances? Explain.

6. How would you describe the biblical concept of joy? What is its source?

7. When was the last time you treated someone as a means to an end? Who was it, and what happened?

8. How does the Kingdom of God affect how we should treat each other?

APPLICATION

Take a moment to pray and ask God, "Is there anyone I need to treat differently?" Maybe it's someone you need to apologize to, someone you need to affirm, or someone you need to serve. Who is it, and what is God asking you to do?

SUMMARY

WEEK THREE

When we set aside our preferences in order to love and serve others, like Jesus, we help make the Kingdom real to others in a way they can receive it. The Kingdom produces righteousness, peace, and joy in the Holy Spirit.

HOW DOES THE KINGDOM OF GOD *CHANGE* OUR RELATIONSHIPS?

PASSAGE:
COLOSSIANS 1:13-14

MEMORY VERSE:
COLOSSIANS 3:13

PAGES 75-88

CONCEPT

We have lost a lot of common ground. There aren't many shared spaces left where people with a variety of perspectives can respectfully interact with each other.

Our lives have become so polarized. We're not always brave enough to say it, but many people spend a good percentage of their day thinking this way:

- **You're for me or you're against me.**
- **I'm right and you're wrong.**
- **My group is the best and your group is the worst.**

This impacts all of us. Technology has accentuated our ability to amplify the voices we agree with and mute the ones we disagree with. If we're inclined (and most people are), it has become safe and simple to live in an echo chamber.

The technical term for this is "confirmation bias." We may have good intentions. Our goal may be to preserve the integrity of our convictions. The problem is, we can easily begin to treat people who see things differently as something less than a person created in the image of God.

How do you disrupt this cycle? You remember that you're a citizen of a different kingdom. In God's Kingdom, our fight is not with people. God loves people—even the ones who disagree with Him.

The religious leaders accused Jesus of being a friend of sinners. Jesus loved people who made mistakes and didn't see things the right way. But He was not a friend of sin; He never weakened His convictions about holiness or how God has called us to live.

Jesus' disciples included a tax collector named Matthew and a zealot named Simon. They were political enemies. Zealots wanted to forcefully overthrow the government, while tax collectors partnered with the Romans to collect money from their own people.

How did these polar opposites coexist? Because both of them had become members of a new kingdom.

When Jesus preaches the "good news" of the Kingdom, He begins with repentance. This is how the Kingdom works. God gives us the opportunity to change our minds. He invites us to turn from the life we're living in pursuit of our own kingdom, to be welcomed into His Kingdom—the life we were created to live.

While we were enemies, aliens, strangers, foreigners, and hostile to God's Kingdom, out of His love and goodness, He offered us the opportunity to be forgiven and welcomed into His family.

We are prone to forget this, but as members of His family, it has to impact the way we treat others.

Being a part of God's Kingdom means we are willing to offer the same forgiveness we have received.

MATTHEW 11:19
The Son of Man came eating and drinking, and they say, "Here is a glutton and a drunkard, a friend of tax collectors and sinners." But wisdom is proved right by her deeds.

COLOSSIANS 1:21
Once you were alienated from God and were enemies in your minds because of your evil behavior.

EPHESIANS 2:19
Consequently, you are no longer foreigners and strangers, but fellow citizens with God's people and also members of his household...

PASSAGE

IN CONTEXT

The book of Colossians is a letter from the apostle Paul to the church in Colossae. This was a healthy church with a genuine faith whose reputation was impacting those around them. However, an ungodly philosophy was passing through the region, so Paul wrote to remind them to look to Jesus.

In this respect, the ancient world was similar to our world— groups of people with different worldviews, attitudes, perspectives, and allegiances to rival kingdoms, all living next door to each other.

Colossians chapter 1 eloquently reinforces the supremacy (He's better than everything else) and the sufficiency (He's all you need) of Christ.

Paul tells them that he hasn't stopped praying for them since he first heard about what God was doing through them. The word was out that they had put their faith in God and were known for their love for all God's people. Paul prays that they would live a life worthy of the Lord and would please Him in every way.

What is happening through the people of this church is no small thing. It is making an impact in the lives of people around them. It is disrupting and threatening the other kingdoms. Paul is asking God to fill them with His strength so they might have endurance and patience as they continue to give thanks to the Father.

Paul then reminds them (and us) of what brought them into the Kingdom and how it should dictate the way they treat others. Kingdoms take after the nature and character of the king.

Read Colossians 1:13-14 on page 80.

COLOSSIANS 1:13-14

[13] For he has rescued us from the dominion of darkness and brought us into the kingdom of the Son he loves, [14] in whom we have redemption, the forgiveness of sins.

WHAT DOES THIS MEAN FOR *US?*

▶▶ Becoming a part of the Kingdom is bigger than joining a church or learning spiritual information. Verse 13 doesn't say we've been educated—it says we've been rescued. We were in a kingdom ruled by darkness, and through Jesus, we've been rescued and brought into a new Kingdom.

This new Kingdom belongs to Jesus. What an incredible picture of the Kingdom. How does Paul describe it? Judgment? Holiness? Power? Those are all included, but the primary lens He wants us to see through is the Kingdom of the Son who God loves.

Jesus is the King of this Kingdom, and He is our only way in. We can't earn our way in, so it can't be taken from us. He redeems us, which means He paid the debt of sin we could never repay.

He lived the perfect life we couldn't live and died a death in our place that we deserved. He sets us free from guilt and shame because He forgave us and made us whole.

And because He is our King, He calls us to live like Him.

When we forget or lose sight of how essential forgiveness is to the Kingdom of God, we've moved on to a different kingdom.

Because we've been forgiven, we forgive. Not because the other person deserves it. Not because they've earned it. Not because they won't ever make another mistake.

When we forgive others, we are not endorsing their behavior or bad decisions. Forgiveness is more than forgetting, because, without forgiveness, those bad feelings can return. Forgiveness does not always lead to reconciliation. Forgiveness does not mean we stay in a dangerous situation.

Forgiveness means we consciously choose to say no to bitterness or offense, and to trust God to make the situation right.

Forgiveness keeps us from living angry and frustrated. It helps us break free from our polarized world. It frees us from feeling like we have to make sure no one gets away with anything. It allows us to have grace and kindness toward people who do not think or live as we do.

Until we're willing to forgive others, our relationships will always be shaky. But once we commit to a lifestyle of forgiveness, we lean into the unshakable Kingdom of the God who forgave us.

WHAT DO I DO WITH THIS?

Do you struggle with guilt and shame? Are you trying to earn the love and approval of Jesus?

When we understand that Jesus offers His forgiveness right where we are—not after we've cleaned ourselves up—we don't have to live tormented by guilt and shame.

Why is forgiving others difficult? Do you want people to get what they deserve? Does it make you feel like a doormat?

When we remember how gracious and forgiving Jesus has been to us, it frees us to forgive others.

Do you find yourself getting angry and upset with people who think and live differently than you? Do you ever find yourself stuck in an echo chamber or dealing with confirmation bias?

Remember, in the Kingdom of God, our fight is not with people. We're called to love our neighbors while we hold on to our convictions.

COLOSSIANS 3:13

Bear with each other and forgive one another if any of you has a grievance against someone. Forgive as the Lord forgave you.

DISCUSSION

1. How polarized has our culture become? What are some things that have caused the polarization?

2. How is God's Kingdom different from the polarization of our culture?

3. Read Colossians 1:13-14. What does verse 13 say we were rescued from? What does each word in that phrase make you think about?

4. What actions, attitudes, and beliefs would characterize a "dominion of darkness"?

5. Read Colossians 1:13-14 again. What does verse 14 say we have in Jesus?

6. What has Jesus redeemed and forgiven you for? Be specific.

7. Do you ever struggle with receiving forgiveness from God? Explain.

8. Do you ever struggle with forgiving others? Explain.

APPLICATION

Is there anything you need to release to God right now? Maybe it's guilt for something you've done, or maybe it's releasing forgiveness for something that was done to you. Take a moment to talk to God about it. What is He saying to you right now? What do you need to do about it?

SUMMARY

WEEK FOUR

We are citizens of a different Kingdom, which begins with repentance and forgiveness. We are forgiven to enter the Kingdom. Our King died so that we could be forgiven, and called us to forgive and love others—forgiveness is essential to the Kingdom.

HOW DOES THE KINGDOM OF GOD *MEET* OUR NEEDS?

PASSAGES:
MATTHEW 6:25-33,
LUKE 12:22-32

MEMORY VERSE:
PHILIPPIANS 4:19

PAGES 89-102

CONCEPT

No matter how much we have, human beings worry about not having enough. We watch financial markets, we check our accounts, we stress about the economy, and we make plans to buy a house or to pay for weddings, college, and retirement.

This is an expected, normal part of our daily lives.

Many people chase a number. They think, *If I can just get to this place, then I'll be free from worry.* The challenging irony is, the more you have, the more you worry about the possibility of losing what you worked so hard to acquire.

There is no number high enough to give us total security and safety. That's what we really want. We want the assurance that everything is going to be alright.

God knows no matter what season of life we're in, we're thinking about provision. *Am I going to have everything I need?*

He does not promise that putting our trust in Him will mean there won't be difficult moments or challenges. But He does promise to meet all of our needs when we put His Kingdom first in our lives.

Jesus addresses this issue in His largest sermon. In order to accommodate the large crowd and to benefit from the natural acoustics, He preached it on the side of a mountain. This is why it's commonly called "The Sermon on the Mount."

It's the longest continuous message we have—the most famous message ever preached—and it's still finding an audience thousands of years later.

We worry as much today as they did then. But in the ancient world, safety and security were harder to find. They didn't have a bank to keep track of their money. Basic necessities were more difficult. They didn't have Costco, a grocery store, a pantry, or even a fridge. Most people ate one meal a day because it took the whole day to make it.

That's why Jesus told them to trust God for their daily bread. They had to work each day to receive it.

MATTHEW 6:11
Give us today our daily bread.

How does the Kingdom impact provision? Jesus says that we're not to worry about our needs, because if we put the Kingdom first, He promises to meet them.

Our life feels shaky when we don't feel like we have what we need. This promise from God allows us to trust in His unshakable provision and His willingness to meet our needs.

PASSAGE

Luke and Matthew present the Sermon on the Mount differently. Matthew writes it consecutively in chapters 5-7. Luke splits the same core material between a smaller passage in 6:20-49 (often called "The Sermon on the Plain" because it takes place on a flat or level field) and chapters 11-12.

Both passages are preceded by Jesus instructing the crowd not to store up treasures for themselves but instead to store up treasure in heaven by investing their resources in the Kingdom of God.

In Matthew, Jesus explains that because our treasure and our hearts are connected, we can't serve both God and money. In Luke, Jesus tells a story about a rich man who has so much that he tears down his storage barns to build bigger ones. God confronts the man immediately because he stored everything up for himself instead of being rich toward God.

Read Matthew 6:25-33 and Luke 12:22-32 on pages 93-94.

MATT. 6:25-33 & LUKE 12:22-32

MATTHEW 6:25-33

[25] "Therefore I tell you, do not worry about your life, what you will eat or drink; or about your body, what you will wear. Is not life more than food, and the body more than clothes? [26] Look at the birds of the air; they do not sow or reap or store away in barns, and yet your heavenly Father feeds them. Are you not much more valuable than they? [27] Can any one of you by worrying add a single hour to your life?

[28] "And why do you worry about clothes? See how the flowers of the field grow. They do not labor or spin. [29] Yet I tell you that not even Solomon in all his splendor was dressed like one of these. [30] If that is how God clothes the grass of the field, which is here today and tomorrow is thrown into the fire, will he not much more clothe you—you of little faith? [31] So do not worry, saying, 'What shall we eat?' or 'What shall we drink?' or 'What shall we wear?' [32] For the pagans run after all these things, and your heavenly Father knows that you need them. [33] But seek first his kingdom and his righteousness, and all these things will be given to you as well."

LUKE 12:22-32

22 Then Jesus said to his disciples: "Therefore I tell you, do not worry about your life, what you will eat; or about your body, what you will wear. 23 For life is more than food, and the body more than clothes. 24 Consider the ravens: They do not sow or reap, they have no storeroom or barn; yet God feeds them. And how much more valuable you are than birds! 25 Who of you by worrying can add a single hour to your life? 26 Since you cannot do this very little thing, why do you worry about the rest?

27 "Consider how the wild flowers grow. They do not labor or spin. Yet I tell you, not even Solomon in all his splendor was dressed like one of these. 28 If that is how God clothes the grass of the field, which is here today, and tomorrow is thrown into the fire, how much more will he clothe you—you of little faith!

29 And do not set your heart on what you will eat or drink; do not worry about it. 30 For the pagan world runs after all such things, and your Father knows that you need them. 31 But seek his kingdom, and these things will be given to you as well.

32 "Do not be afraid, little flock, for your Father has been pleased to give you the kingdom."

WHAT DOES THIS MEAN FOR *US?*

> > > Both passages start with "Therefore…" to point us back to the previous thought. If you make storing up treasures for yourself your goal, you'll always be worried. When you are the king of your own kingdom, you are ultimately dependent on yourself for provision.

No matter how much we're able to accumulate, there is no magic number we can get to in order to make us feel safe.

When you give up your kingdom in exchange for the Kingdom of God, you are no longer king, but you're also no longer your source of provision. God promises to meet your needs. This is why He tells us not to worry.

God knows we worry. It comes naturally to us. It robs us of our joy and peace. Worry takes us out of the present and gives us panic and fear about our future.

Jesus reminds us how important we are to God. When He points to the birds of the air (or ravens) and the wildflowers, these were things the crowd could immediately see. It did not take any

imagination to understand how well God provided for them and how little time they spent worrying about not having enough.

Once again, Jesus is going all the way ◀ back to the first chapter of the Bible where we first discover the concept of Kingdom. He gives Adam the responsibility to rule over the animals, to ensure they're cared for the way God cares for him, because this is what it means to be in the Kingdom.

Even when Adam and Eve failed to care for the animals through their disobedience, God remained faithful to them.

This is the same concept Jesus is alluding to when He says the pagans worry about what they'll eat or wear and that they run after all these things. Remember back to the Intro Week 1, where we learned the ancient world was filled with tribal gods. You never knew how they felt about you. All of your sacrifices were done to please them so your crops would grow and you would have what you needed.

Jesus is saying, "You don't have to perform religious rituals to get the gods to notice you. That's a miserable way to live. It leads to uncertainty and fear."

When we put our trust in anything other than God—a religious system, our career, the economy, our political party, the stock market—we are left to fend for ourselves. The outcome is always the same: we live in constant worry no matter how much we have.

Jesus is offering us a better way.

Notice the last line in the Luke passage: "Do not be afraid, little flock." Jesus references Psalm 23 and takes on the role of the shepherd who cares for His sheep. Because of the shepherd, the sheep don't have to worry if they'll be taken care of.

He continues to say that the Father has been pleased to give you the Kingdom. Sometimes Kingdom language sounds official and political. Again, Jesus brings it back to familial language and the Father heart of God. He's not mad or bothered by us and our needs. He's not surprised when we worry about where our provision and our security will come from.

God knows we think about these things. He doesn't want us to worry because He's pleased, He's willing, and He's excited to give us the Kingdom and everything we could ever need. That's His heart toward us.

He wants us to trust Him. He wants us to know He's not holding out on us. There's not a better version out there that would be more fulfilling if we made it happen in our own strength.

But we don't receive this kind of confidence with a partial commitment. He gives the Kingdom to those who seek it first above all the other options. This is not about what we do but ultimately who we trust.

GENESIS 1:26
Then God said, "Let us make mankind in our image, in our likeness, so that they may rule over the fish in the sea and the birds in the sky, over the livestock and all the wild animals, and over all the creatures that move along the ground."

PSALM 23:1
The Lord is my shepherd, I lack nothing.

WHAT DO I DO WITH THIS?

Are you storing up treasures for yourself because you believe you are your source? Do you constantly stress over your resources, your investments, your career, and the economy?

Seeking God's Kingdom first does not mean you don't make wise financial choices. It does not mean you don't invest as a good steward, manage your resources, and plan for your financial future.

But those things are not your source. God is your source.

When you're rich toward God—when you seek His Kingdom first—you can have the confidence to know He'll meet all your needs. His provision is not up and down like our businesses, our economy, or our investment markets. We can't take any of those with us anyway.

What makes it difficult for you to trust God as your source?

How would you live differently if you trusted Him?

PHILIPPIANS 4:19

And my God will meet all your needs according to the riches of his glory in Christ Jesus.

DISCUSSION

1. How often do you struggle with worry or fear? Explain.

2. What are some things that cause you to worry?

3. Read Matthew 6:33. What does it mean to "seek first" God's Kingdom?

4. According to Matthew 6:33, what happens when you seek God's Kingdom first? Do you believe this is true? Explain.

5. Where do you typically look for security or provision?

6. Why is it difficult to trust God as your source?

7. How would trusting God as your source affect your life?

8. Read Luke 12:32. Why do you think Jesus brings us back to a shepherding image here? What does this image communicate?

APPLICATION

Did God reveal anything through this chapter that you need to surrender? Is there anything you need to reprioritize? Talk to Him about it. What will you do as a result?

SUMMARY

WEEK FIVE

God's Kingdom offers us an amazing promise: if we seek the Kingdom first, above all else, He will provide everything we need. The Kingdom is a promise that when we trust God as our source, we have a King who provides and meets our needs.

WHY IS IT AN "ALREADY-NOT-YET-KINGDOM"?

PASSAGE:
LUKE 23:38-43

MEMORY VERSE:
REVELATION 22:20

PAGES 103-118

CONCEPT

Most people do not enjoy tension. Tension in a relationship can be stressful. Tension in our bodies may lead to soreness and even pain.

But when it's leveraged the right way, tension can produce incredible growth. Without tension, our muscles don't grow. Without the tension of intellectual difficulty, we don't get smarter.

And tension in a relationship can produce clarifying conversations that result in far greater intimacy and genuine connection.

God is comfortable with tension. He knows how to leverage it to help us grow.

Perhaps nowhere is this tension more real than in our understanding of the Kingdom of God.

Think about this: If Jesus preached that the Kingdom has come, if He told His disciples to preach the Kingdom, and if that's what the early church preached, why does it feel like the Kingdom is not fully here?

If the arrival of the Kingdom means God's rule and reign are here, why is the world still so messed up?

- **Why do the righteous suffer?**
- **Why do the wicked seem to thrive?**
- **Why do evil and injustice not only exist but mock the things of God?**

I'm guessing you've asked these questions too. You're not alone and you're not wrong. Questions like these have created tension for humanity as long as we've been around.

At least 16 times in the book of Psalms, the phrase "How long…" is repeated. "How long will you forget us, Lord, how long do we have to wait, how long will the enemy mock you, how long will you hide your face…"

When Jesus preaches the Kingdom by saying that the time has come, He's answering this "how long" question.

Heaven has said, "Wait no longer; the time has come." Heaven heard your "how longs" and the answer is "No longer."

But if this is the case, why do some days feel like we're singing the same old "how long" songs?

Bible scholars describe this tension as the "Already-Not-Yet-Kingdom."

Both of these things are true at the same time.

Jesus did bring His Kingdom.

- **He preached this message and invited us into His family.**
- **He healed the sick.**

PSALM 6:3
My soul is in deep anguish. How long, Lord, how long?

PSALM 13:1
How long, Lord? Will you forget me forever? How long will you hide your face from me?

PSALM 35:17
How long, Lord, will you look on? Rescue me from their ravages, my precious life from these lions.

PSALM 79:5
How long, Lord? Will you be angry forever? How long will your jealousy burn like fire?

PSALM 89:46
How long, Lord? Will you hide yourself forever? How long will your wrath burn like fire?

PSALM 119:84
How long must your servant wait? When will you punish my persecutors?

- **He performed miracles and cast out demons.**
- **He paid the debt of sin through His death on the cross.**
- **He triumphed over the grave through His resurrection.**
- **He gave us His Holy Spirit to empower us.**
- **He built His Church, which is still moving throughout the earth reaching people and building lives.**

We have all benefited from all of these things. They are available to anyone who would receive Him. Our world is not heaven, but through Jesus and His Kingdom, heaven breaks through and shows up on earth on a regular basis.

And yet our world is still filled with sin, wickedness, injustice, and evil. That's the "not-yet" part.

Why would Jesus do this? Not because He's okay with sin, wickedness, injustice, and evil. He came to destroy those things.

The reason Jesus waits to bring His Kingdom in its fullness is because He's not done adding to His family. We live with tension so His Kingdom can continue to expand.

This is more than praying a salvation prayer. It's the whole package.

When the Kingdom comes into a person's heart, it changes their whole life.

As we've learned, when the Kingdom comes into a person's heart, it changes their whole life. They're no longer the center of their world. They love others; they serve; they forgive; righteousness, peace, and joy fill their life; and they trust God as their source, so they live generously.

Jesus tells a parable about this tension where a man sowed a field of wheat but his enemy came at night and mixed in weeds. The servants asked the man if they should rip out the weeds, but the man said, let the two of them grow together so none of the wheat gets pulled out. Jesus told His disciples that this parable is about the end of the age when He would come back to judge the world.

Matthew 24 is one of Jesus' longest teachings about the end of history. As you might imagine, people had all kinds of questions and wild speculations—just like we have today. There are two significant things Jesus says very clearly without mystery or conspiracy.

First, He says this gospel of the Kingdom will be preached to the whole world as a testimony to the nations, and then the end shall come. In other words, everyone gets the invitation. History will continue until the whole world gets the opportunity. No one will be able to say, "I didn't know."

MATTHEW 24:14
And this gospel of the kingdom will be preached in the whole world as a testimony to all nations, and then the end will come.

And second, only the Father knows when that final day will come. The clear implication is that God doesn't want us sitting around waiting for it but to continue to advance His Kingdom throughout the earth. The end will take care of itself.

MATTHEW 24:36
But about that day or hour no one knows, not even the angels in heaven, nor the Son, but only the Father.

We do not need to be worried or afraid about His return, judgment, and the end of history. When the world starts shaking, we have the confidence of being part of a Kingdom that can never be shaken.

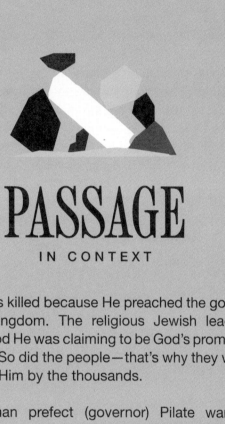

PASSAGE

IN CONTEXT

DANIEL 7:13-14

13 In my vision at night I looked, and there before me was one like a son of man, coming with the clouds of heaven. He approached the Ancient of Days and was led into his presence. 14 He was given authority, glory and sovereign power; all nations and peoples of every language worshiped him. His dominion is an everlasting dominion that will not pass away, and his kingdom is one that will never be destroyed.

Jesus was killed because He preached the gospel of the Kingdom. The religious Jewish leaders understood He was claiming to be God's promised Messiah. So did the people—that's why they were following Him by the thousands.

The Roman prefect (governor) Pilate wanted to let Jesus go but the angry crowds wouldn't listen. Jesus was beaten and dragged through the streets. The religious leaders sneered at Him and mocked Him. The soldiers taunted Him and took His clothes.

There were two criminals next to Him when He was crucified. Crucifixion was so humiliating and painful, it was reserved only for the worst rebels, criminals, and slaves. More than just killing the person, it was designed as torture, and it was meant to set a horrifying example and intimidate everyone who saw it into obedience.

No king would be subjected to obedience. And certainly no king would respond the way Jesus did. He forgave them even as they mocked and killed Him.

Read Luke 23:38-43 on page 110. ⟶

Luke ties Jesus' identity as King to the reason He was killed. The contrast between the two criminals provides a snapshot of two extreme responses. One is to mock Jesus—think about the fact His name is still used as a curse word around the world today. The second is to worship Him—thousands of years later He gains new worshipers on a daily basis around the world.

The second criminal believes Jesus is a King and asks Him to remember Him when He comes into His Kingdom.

Jesus tells him, "...today you will be with me in paradise." There is great significance in these eight words.

All the criminal did was believe in Jesus and receive it as a gift. Jesus tells this man, "Today." There is no delay. His Kingdom has come and can be entered. And finally, the Kingdom is paradise—the same word used for both the Garden of Eden and heaven. Paradise is anywhere the reign of God has come in its fullness.

LUKE 23:38-43

[38] There was a written notice above him, which read: THIS IS THE KING OF THE JEWS.

[39] One of the criminals who hung there hurled insults at him: "Aren't you the Messiah? Save yourself and us!"

[40] But the other criminal rebuked him. "Don't you fear God," he said, "since you are under the same sentence? [41] We are punished justly, for we are getting what our deeds deserve. But this man has done nothing wrong."

[42] Then he said, "Jesus, remember me when you come into your kingdom."

[43] Jesus answered him, "Truly I tell you, today you will be with me in paradise."

WHAT DOES THIS MEAN FOR *US?*

2 PETER 3:9

The Lord is not slow in keeping his promise, as some understand slowness. Instead he is patient with you, not wanting anyone to perish, but everyone to come to repentance.

This is an extreme salvation story. This is not ideal. Most of us do not give our lives to Christ in the moments right before we pass from this world.

But it does give us an excellent window into the heart of God, who doesn't want anyone to perish but for everyone to come to repentance.

This is the "Already-Not-Yet-Kingdom."

This criminal experienced the fullness of the Kingdom on that same day. The rest of Jesus' followers received it gradually. They lived incredible lives and saw thousands of people impacted by the message of Jesus. They also saw all kinds of sin, wickedness, and challenges—and God's faithfulness overcame it all.

If we were to speculate, if the criminal had lived, Jesus likely would have told him to get with the disciples, to make disciples, to build the Church, and to advance the Kingdom.

The same is true for us. If you've lost a loved one who was a follower of Christ, they are experiencing the fullness of the Kingdom while your understanding is continuing to gradually grow.

This is the tension Jesus set up in His Kingdom.

The Kingdom of God came through the person of Jesus for the whole world to receive. The Kingdom continues to come in and through His people. And the Kingdom will be consummated at Christ's return.

It doesn't matter which nation on earth has the biggest empire or military superpower. It doesn't matter who's been elected or who is in control. No circumstance can stop it. On that day, every knee in heaven, on earth, and under the earth is going to bow and every tongue is going to confess Jesus is Lord, to the glory of the Father. ◄ ▷

We are not meant to allow the pain, wickedness, and injustice lingering in our world to question the goodness or the character of God. Instead, let it be a reminder there is still work to be done. The Kingdom of Jesus is still advancing. There is time for more people to be added to His family.

In the light of eternity, someday this will all feel like a distant memory. What is eternity going to be like? Just how Jesus wants it. We don't know all the details, but it will be better than we ever imagined.

Jesus said anyone who leaves their home or their family ◄ for the sake of the Kingdom will receive many times as much in the age to come. That's not anti-family—it simply means eternity is going to be amazing for those who prioritized His Kingdom.

When will it come? We don't know. But it will happen right when the Father has chosen. His timing is perfect.

The second to last verse of the Bible is a promise from Jesus to come soon, followed by a common one-word prayer from the early church: "Maranatha." It means "Come, Lord."

PHILIPPIANS 2:9-11
9 Therefore God exalted him to the highest place and gave him the name that is above every name,
10 that at the name of Jesus every knee should bow, in heaven and on earth and under the earth,
11 and every tongue acknowledge that Jesus Christ is Lord, to the glory of God the Father.

▷ **LUKE 18:29-30**
29 "Truly I tell you," Jesus said to them, "no one who has left home or wife or brothers or sisters or parents or children for the sake of the kingdom of God 30 will fail to receive many times as much in this age, and in the age to come eternal life."

WHAT DO I DO WITH THIS?

Do you find yourself getting nervous or worried about the end of the world? Can you be drawn into mysterious conspiracies and speculation?

Remember the guidelines Jesus gave us. The Kingdom delays not so sin and evil can triumph but in order for the Kingdom to advance and for more people to be added to the family. The gospel will be preached to the whole world.

And we won't know the day or the hour.

When we think about His return, according to Jesus, our response should not be speculation and conspiracy but a greater love and urgency to see His message received in the lives of people who do not know Him.

If we will make this our focus, then no matter what earthly kingdoms rise or fall, we won't be shaken.

REVELATION 22:20

He who testifies to these things says, "Yes, I am coming soon." Amen. Come, Lord Jesus.

DISCUSSION

1. The Kingdom of God has been described as an "Already-Not-Yet-Kingdom." How would you explain this phrase in your own words?

2. How have you already experienced the Kingdom of God in your life?

3. In what ways are you waiting for the fullness of God's Kingdom to arrive?

4. Read Luke 23:38-43. Contrast the two criminals who were crucified with Jesus. How did each person respond to God?

5. How does each criminal's response parallel how people respond to Jesus still today?

6. According to what you just read, why has God delayed Jesus' return and the fulfillment of His Kingdom on earth?

7. Read Revelation 22:20. Why do you think the early church anticipated Jesus' return with such eagerness?

8. Are you eagerly anticipating Christ's return? Explain.

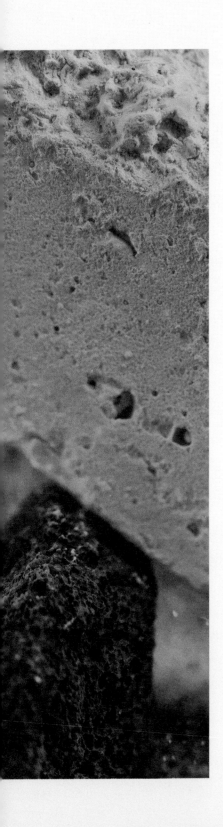

APPLICATION

We are part of an "Already-Not-Yet-Kingdom." This is because God wants everyone to have an opportunity to receive Jesus before He returns. Is there someone in your life who needs to hear about the love and goodness of God? Write their name below. Will you commit to pray for this person every day? What's something you can do to tell them about God?

SUMMARY

WEEK SIX

Jesus connected His Kingdom and eternity. The Kingdom has come, but there is coming a day when it will come completely. The purpose of waiting is for as many people as possible to be added to His Kingdom.

HOW DOES GOD'S KINGDOM *RESPOND TO* DARKNESS?

PASSAGE:
MATTHEW 16:15-19

MEMORY VERSE:
1 JOHN 4:11-12

PAGES 119-132

CONCEPT

The Kingdom of God challenges empires and rival kingdoms. The earliest Christians said "Jesus is Lord" not only because it was true (and still is) but because it meant Caesar (the Roman Emperor) was not.

There is no king above King Jesus. There is no throne and no name higher than His name. His Kingdom is an everlasting Kingdom that will not pass away.

But as we've learned, this is an "Already-Not-Yet-Kingdom." Wickedness, injustice, and evil still exist in the world. You may be asking yourself:

- **Is the world getting darker?**
- **If so, how do I equip my kids for a culture that is increasingly antagonistic toward my values?**
- **How do I remain steadfast in my convictions in a broken world?**

These are difficult and important questions. How do we respond? This leads us to the really big question: *What do I do as a follower of Christ if the world is getting darker?*

Christians have been wrestling with this for thousands of years. In fact, this was a heated debate in the ancient world Jesus grew up in. There were groups of people who were committed to different strategies. They all wanted Jesus to join their team. He regularly failed to meet their expectations as He made His own path in obedience to His Father and in demonstration of this new Kingdom.

The Essenes passionately believed the world was irredeemably broken, so their response was to withdraw from society and live in seclusion. The Zealots felt the culture was so dark that it justified taking up arms to fight. The Sadducees were religious leaders who tried to preserve power through the political system. The Herodians were Jews who supported the Roman government. Each of these groups held strong religious and political convictions, often in conflict with each other.

One of the most helpful theological studies on this subject is *Christ and Culture* by Richard Niebuhr. It's a theological textbook, but his basic premise is that there are three primary responses to culture: reject, receive, and redeem.

How do we know what to do with different aspects of culture: getting a tattoo, using curse words, drugs, alcohol, dancing, gambling, what we read and watch, or how we vote?

As followers of Christ, how do we know which things to reject (have nothing to do with), which things to receive (we are free to enjoy), and which things to redeem (engage in once they've been transformed to honor and reflect God's Kingdom)?

PASSAGE

IN CONTEXT

You may not realize it, but one of the most important moments in the Bible takes place at one of the darkest places in their culture. Caesarea Philippi was a lush garden spring located about 40 miles north of the Sea of Galilee. Temples were built at this site, and it was used in all sorts of lewd pagan festivals, including sexual immorality and even human sacrifice.

This place was unholy, the kind of place a good Jew would never go. This is why the disciples were shocked when Jesus took them there to have one of His most critical conversations. Jesus took them there to ask them who He really was and to tell them the one thing He promised to build.

All of this was on purpose. The implication was clear. No matter how dark the culture was, no matter how wicked and unholy things grew, the Church, the expression of God's Kingdom, would move forward.

Read Matthew 16:15-19 on page 124.

Jesus said He would build His Church on the rock of the revelation that He is the Messiah, the Son of the living God. The darkest forces of hell itself cannot overcome it. And He gave the keys of the Kingdom—the authority, the ability to lock and unlock, to receive and reject—to His people.

MATTHEW 16:15-19

[15] "But what about you?" he asked. "Who do you say I am?"

[16] Simon Peter answered, "You are the Messiah, the Son of the living God."

[17] Jesus replied, "Blessed are you, Simon son of Jonah, for this was not revealed to you by flesh and blood, but by my Father in heaven. [18] And I tell you that you are Peter, and on this rock I will build my church, and the gates of Hades will not overcome it. [19] I will give you the keys of the kingdom of heaven; whatever you bind on earth will be bound in heaven, and whatever you loose on earth will be loosed in heaven."

WHAT DOES THIS MEAN FOR *US?*

> > > First and foremost, we take comfort in the fact Jesus was not unaware of the depths of wickedness and evil human beings are capable of. He knew His Church, the expression of His Kingdom, would not only survive cultural darkness but overcome and change it.

Next, we remember this discussion plays out over the course of the New Testament. The early church struggled with which parts of the Jewish law followers of Christ needed to follow, which cultural practices to keep, and which ones to avoid.

By the time we get to Acts 15, under the direction of the Holy Spirit, the disciples decided new believers did not need to be circumcised or follow the law of Moses. The only thing they insisted on was not to eat food dedicated to idols and to avoid sexual immorality (any sexual activity outside of a husband and wife in marriage).

▶ God gives us the freedom to make choices while always offering His wisdom and the leading of His Holy Spirit. However, we should remember there are at least three times in the New Testament where a list of consistent, unrepentant behaviors appears to disqualify us from the inheritance of the Kingdom of God (see 1 Corinthians 6:9-10, Galatians 5:19-21, Ephesians 5:3-5).

In each of the lists, sexual immorality is prominent because this impulse is strong and driven by a desire to please ourselves above everything else. This attitude is fundamentally opposed to the Kingdom.

It's easy to get to a place where we think it's loving to let people follow their hearts or do what is accepted by current cultural opinions. It's not our job to correct people who don't care what we think, but when we're invited, we need to speak with both love and truth.

Avoiding an unpopular yet biblical perspective is not loving. At the same time, we build trust when we're quick to clarify the difference between a biblical mandate and our personal opinion. These two things are not equal.

And in our own lives, we don't start with "What do I get to do?" We start with "What is going to encourage and bless the other people in my life?"

We don't make people accept our personal preferences in order to have a relationship with Jesus. He comes first— our preferences follow.

In week 3, we learned the way of the Kingdom is to set aside our preferences for the sake of loving and serving others. Practically speaking, in areas of conscience, if something you watch, eat, or listen to causes a brother or sister in Christ to struggle in their relationship with God, you don't do it. If going to a particular restaurant, participating in a hobby, or voicing a certain political view causes another believer to stumble, you don't do it.

We start with "How can I prioritize God's Kingdom in each of these areas of my life?" We start with what the Word says. We ask trusted voices. We consider how our attitudes in these areas of our lives are impacting others.

When we're concerned about the darkness, we don't shout at it. We shine our light in the darkness.

If we want to transfer our values to the people we love and care about the most, we have to invite them into the process.

- **Do the people in our lives experience God's love through the way we live?**
- **Do our views allow us to use our gifts to serve people? Not just in the way we like to serve, but in a way that adds value to them?**
- **Are we inviting our kids or younger people into the process to help them take their next step? This is how discipleship works.**

EPHESIANS 5:3-5
3 But among you there must not be even a hint of sexual immorality, or of any kind of impurity, or of greed, because these are improper for God's holy people.
4 Nor should there be obscenity, foolish talk or coarse joking, which are out of place, but rather thanksgiving.
5 For of this you can be sure: No immoral, impure or greedy person—such a person is an idolater—has any inheritance in the kingdom of Christ and of God.

1 CORINTHIANS 10:23-24
23 "I have the right to do anything," you say— but not everything is beneficial. "I have the right to do anything"— but not everything is constructive.
24 No one should seek their own good, but the good of others.

WHAT DO I DO WITH THIS?

God wants you to have conviction about your preferences. But what we watch, what we eat, our hobbies, our political attitudes, and our opinions should help people feel closer to God, not further away.

Do you invite God to speak to you and challenge your perspectives and preferences?

Which has a bigger impact on how you see things: the Word or the attitudes and opinions of culture?

Are you quick to clarify the difference between biblical truth and your personal opinion?

Challenging someone's deeply held personal opinions and cultural attitudes doesn't happen immediately. And it only happens when the other person knows we genuinely love them. It also requires time and trust. We have to allow the Holy Spirit to lead in the process. This is how light shines into cultural darkness.

1 JOHN 4:11-12

[11] Dear friends, since God so loved us, we also ought to love one another. [12] No one has ever seen God; but if we love one another, God lives in us and his love is made complete in us.

DISCUSSION

THE FOLLOWING QUESTIONS WILL HELP YOU PROCESS
THE CHAPTER AND APPLY IT TO YOUR LIFE. ANSWER THEM
ON YOUR OWN OR PRIOR TO YOUR SMALL GROUP MEETING.

1. In what ways do you see "darkness" at work in our culture today?

2. Read Matthew 16:15-19. Why would Jesus take His disciples to Caesarea Philippi to have this important conversation with them? What is the significance of that location?

3. What did Jesus declare about the Church in this passage?

4. When the Kingdom of God comes into contact with culture, we have three choices: reject, receive, or redeem. How would you describe the differences between these choices?

5. How can we determine whether a behavior or activity is acceptable and beneficial? Where can we turn for guidance?

6. Read 1 Corinthians 10:23-24. What does this verse mean for our actions and personal preferences? What should govern our decisions?

7. Look up 1 Corinthians 6:9-10, Galatians 5:19-21, and Ephesians 5:3-5 in the Bible. What do these verses have in common? What stands out to you?

8. Why does sexual immorality contradict the values of the Kingdom of God so much?

APPLICATION

Spend a few minutes to reflect and pray about this chapter. Do you have any activities, hobbies, or personal preferences that should change? What impact are they having on the people around you? Do they reflect God to others?

SUMMARY

WEEK SEVEN

The Kingdom shines God's light into the darkness of the world. Because Jesus is above culture, when the Kingdom comes into contact with the culture, we have the choice to reject, receive, or redeem. We don't do this based on our personal preferences but to love and serve others.

HOW DOES GOD'S KINGDOM *IMPACT* MY FAMILY?

PASSAGE:
1 THESSALONIANS 2:10-12

MEMORY VERSE:
1 THESSALONIANS 5:11

PAGES 133-148

CONCEPT

If the Kingdom of God makes a difference anywhere, the place where we want it to start is in our home.

Home is the place where we are most known. Home is the place where opinions matter the most. The agreement of acquaintances and strangers on social media cannot undo the relational disagreements we have at home.

Our careers and our work can be great. Our hobbies may flourish as we cross things off our life goals or bucket list. But if things are not good at home, it feels like our whole world is falling apart.

The people who love us the most can also cause the greatest amount of pain. And it's hard to grow in the Kingdom of God when it feels like everything at home is shaking.

This is especially true for parents. There is no pain like "kid pain." Any parent who loves their children would much rather personally endure challenges in their own lives than have to sit back and watch their kids struggle.

The primary way God wants us to understand His Kingdom is not as an army, not as a political "nation-state," not as a religious organization, but as a family.

Of all the ways He could have identified Himself— Creator, Judge, Lord, or King—God chose "Father." He is all of those things and more, but the primary way He relates to us is as Father. It's how He relates to Jesus. God builds everything through the family.

◀ ▶ **1 CORINTHIANS 1:3**
Grace and peace to you from God our Father and the Lord Jesus Christ.

Family is the fundamental building block of humanity. None of us choose our family but all of us are shaped by family. Everyone has their own experience and opinion of what it should look like.

And we've never had more access to all these opinions. Anyone with a smartphone or a YouTube channel can declare themselves an expert and begin to give all kinds of advice and input on what the family should look like.

The results of this approach have been devastating.

Culture has elevated personal expression and individual happiness above everything else. We should not be surprised that when we make "follow your heart," "live your truth," and "don't let anyone tell you who to love" the guiding cultural values, we end up lonely, isolated, dissatisfied, and unfulfilled.

When parents tell their children, "You can do whatever makes you happy," it ends up in chaos. Especially when the parents are living by the same principles.

This is not to suggest God is anti-happiness. No one is more committed to building loving and healthy families than He is. Ephesians 3:14-15 tells us every family on earth gets their name from Him—He has a loving plan

▶ **EPHESIANS 3:14-15**
14 For this reason I kneel before the Father, 15 from whom every family in heaven and on earth derives its name.

GENESIS 2:24

That is why a man leaves his father and mother and is united to his wife, and they become one flesh.

MATTHEW 19:5

For this reason a man will leave his father and mother and be united to his wife, and the two will become one flesh.

EPHESIANS 5:31

For this reason a man will leave his father and mother and be united to his wife, and the two will become one flesh.

for every single family no matter how many challenges they face.

But God's pattern is different. In Genesis 2:24, He said a man would leave his father and mother and be joined with his wife and the two would become one. This is His pattern. Both Jesus and Paul point to this passage because this family model is consistent throughout the whole Bible.

Ephesians 5 shows us that husbands are to love their wives like Jesus loves His Church. This is where our example comes from. This kind of love does not promote itself or its own interests but always defers and always considers the other, because it's not searching for fulfillment from a spouse or even our own emotions.

Like everything else in the Kingdom, our source is God Himself. He alone can give us the love and power to experience the Kingdom in our homes. If we wait for our families to act the way we want them to, we'll always be frustrated. Even the most disciplined and loving among us cannot do it over the long term with our own willpower.

PASSAGE

IN CONTEXT

This passage comes from a letter from the apostle Paul to the church in Thessalonica. This was a great church known for its love for others. They didn't just talk about Jesus; their lives demonstrated the reality of His power in such a dramatic way, the whole region had heard about the Kingdom of God through their example.

He's writing them a letter to encourage them to keep moving forward, to explain how much he and his fellow leaders loved this church, to prepare them for challenges, and to remind them of Jesus' return at the end of the age.

When Paul wrote to the churches, he consistently used family metaphors. He told the Corinthians they had a lot of teachers but very few fathers, and, in Jesus, he had become a spiritual father to them. In the verses leading up to this passage, Paul told the Thessalonians he cared for them like a nursing mother!

The point is, God wants the people in His Kingdom to relate to each other like a family. To follow His example. These principles help us in all of our relationships, but especially in our homes.

Read 1 Thessalonians 2:10-12 on page 140.

How does a loving father deal with his own children? In other words, what is the culture of a Kingdom home? Encouragement, comfort, and the urge to live a life worthy of God. That's the culture God is calling us to build in our homes.

1 THESSALONIANS
2:10-12

[10] You are witnesses, and so is God, of how holy, righteous and blameless we were among you who believed. [11] For you know that we dealt with each of you as a father deals with his own children, [12] encouraging, comforting and urging you to live lives worthy of God, who calls you into his kingdom and glory.

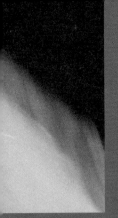

WHAT DOES THIS MEAN FOR *US?*

> > > To experience this culture in our homes, we first have to set God up as King. He is the head of our homes. We want to invite His presence and His Spirit to dwell with us.

Nothing creates disunity faster in a home than when there are different standards. If spouses wait to love, honor, and show respect until they feel loved and respected, they end up in a cold stalemate. But when husbands and wives love and serve each other because of the love and grace they've received from the Father, both of them benefit.

The same is true for children. When Mom and Dad obey God and model what it looks like to love and forgive, the kids view this as the normal way of life. It does not mean their behavior changes, but it does form standards and shape their expectations, even when they can't verbalize it.

This is why it's critical for the home to be filled with God's Word as the standard for everyone. This moves the culture of the home from family tradition to spiritual truth. When the Word is not

prominent in the life of a family, the culture of our homes becomes more connected to our personalities and our preferences.

We are all busy and have full schedules, so it's not realistic to have substantial family Bible study on a daily basis. But if the Word is not discussed, if it does not factor into shaping the values, then its absence will be felt by all.

God's Father-heart is expressed through encouragement, comfort, and the urge to live a life worthy of God. We all need to be reminded of these things every day.

For young families, a simple way to do this is to read the Bible each night when the kids go to bed, even before they're old enough to read. In less than 10 minutes (depending on how good the kids are at stalling), you can build a baseline that will follow them throughout their lives. It also reinforces the routine of talking about God's heart for our family on an ongoing basis.

As the kids get older, the routine of talking about the things of God as a family will continue to develop. Anxiety, insecurity, and the temptations of the world don't come only on Sundays or a few times per year. These are daily struggles, so they need to be met with daily encounters with God's Spirit and His Word.

When the Kingdom of God shapes a family, it does not mean there are no problems or challenges. But it does mean we face those challenges differently. There will be misunderstandings, offenses, frustration and aggravation, and moments of conflict. But forgiveness, the grace of God, and the power of His Spirit can help us rise above these moments.

Face your challenges together as a family. Don't assume the worst. Extend trust. Take the time to listen actively. Make sure honest communication is valued. Processing your emotions is not easy, but it does bring you closer. In all these things, allow God's Word to frame your conversation.

There is no perfect family. None of us have all the answers. That's why spiritual family is so helpful. We do not walk through these moments alone. When our family is connected to a larger spiritual family, we experience peace and grace we cannot produce on our own.

If you're not familiar, when we use the term "spiritual family," we mean that God places us in a local church and connects us to people whom we walk with and relate to as brothers and sisters in Christ.

When our family is connected to a larger spiritual family, we experience peace and grace we cannot produce on our own.

God's Father-heart is expressed through encouragement, comfort, and the urge to live a life worthy of God.

PSALM 68:6a
God sets the lonely in families...

1 CORINTHIANS 12:18
But in fact God has placed the parts in the body, every one of them, just as he wanted them to be.

WHAT DO I DO WITH THIS?

Does your family recognize and honor God as the head of your home? Have you committed to honor and love Him first?

Even if you've made mistakes and you don't know how this works, this is where you have to start.

Have you set God's Word as the standard for your home? Do you find encouragement, comfort, and the urge to live a life worthy of God from the Bible?

Even 5 minutes each day of reading and talking about the Bible will make a big difference. Do not allow guilt or shame to stop you. We all start somewhere. You'll be surprised how quickly things can change.

Have you committed to spiritual family? The relationships we invest in today prepare us for the storms of tomorrow. Being part of a church family is not an obligation; it's one of the primary ways God brings us what we need in life.

1 THESSALONIANS 5:11

Therefore encourage one another and build each other up, just as in fact you are doing.

DISCUSSION

1. The primary way God wants us to understand His Kingdom is as a family. Why is this significant?

2. Read 1 Thessalonians 2:10-12. How does Paul say he dealt with the believers in Thessalonica when he was with them? What did he do for them?

3. How can we encourage others?

4. How can we comfort others?

5. How can we urge someone else to live a life worthy of God?

6. To experience God's Kingdom in our homes, we must first set God up as King. Why is this the first step?

7. To experience God's Kingdom, we must fill our homes with God's Word. What are some practical ways to do this?

8. How does spiritual family play a critical role in establishing God's Kingdom in your home?

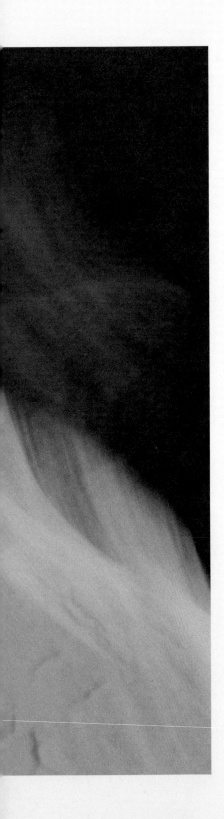

APPLICATION

Take a moment to think about your family:

• **Who needs encouragement?**
• **Who needs comfort?**
• **Who can you urge to live a life worthy of God?**

Write their names below and what they need. Pray for each person. What will you do this week to help them?

SUMMARY

WEEK EIGHT

God is a Father, and He has a clear plan for how families love and serve each other. We do not love people based on what they deserve. We love God through the way we love and serve our family.

THE MEANING
BEHIND THE BRAND
UNSHAKABLE

HEBREWS 12:27b-28

27 ...the removing of what can be shaken—that is, created things—so that what cannot be shaken may remain.
28 Therefore, since we are receiving a kingdom that cannot be shaken, let us be thankful, and so worship God acceptably with reverence and awe...

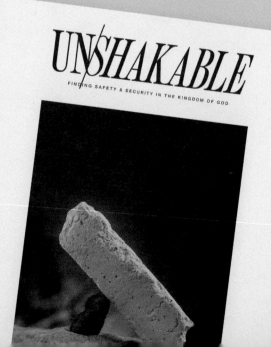

> Hebrews 12:27b-28 explains that God allows things in our lives to shake so the things that can't be shaken (like His Kingdom) remain.

> In one of His most famous parables, Jesus talked about a wise and foolish builder. The wise man built his house on a rock, while the foolish man built on sand. When storms come, a house built on sand falls apart, but the one built on rock isn't shaken.

> The images and textures of rocks and sand throughout this guide are simply meant to reinforce these concepts. We designed this guide with high quality art to inspire you to leave it out on your coffee table, your nightstand, or anywhere it can be a conversation starter.

> This content was written with the goal of being clear enough for someone unfamiliar with the Bible to follow, while also being deep enough to engage a mature believer.

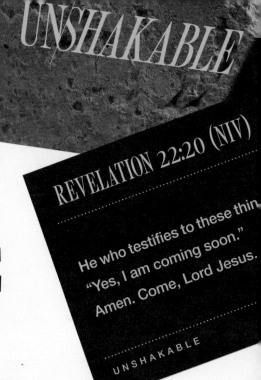

UNSHAKABLE

REVELATION 22:20 (NIV)

He who testifies to these thin[

"Yes, I am coming soon."

Amen. Come, Lord Jesus.

UNSHAKABLE

SCRIPTURE CARDS

These Scripture memory cards** correspond to the memory verse for each week in the *Unshakable* study.

We encourage you to memorize these verses during each week of *Unshakable.* To help, punch out these cards and put them somewhere visible, like the dash of your car, the back of your phone, or your bathroom mirror.

**Scripture memory cards are found in the back of the book.

PSALM 62:1-2 (NIV)

¹ Truly my soul finds rest in God; my salvation comes from him.
² Truly he is my rock and my salvation; he is my fortress, I will never be shaken.

UNSHAKAB[

FOR MORE RESOURCES
VISIT US ONLINE

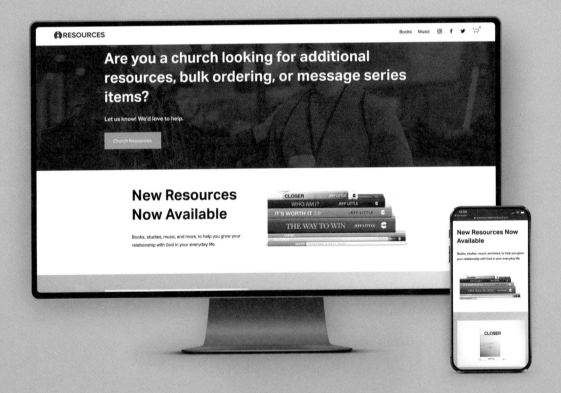

MILESTONERESOURCES.COM

⊖RESOURCES

MILESTONERESOURCES.COM

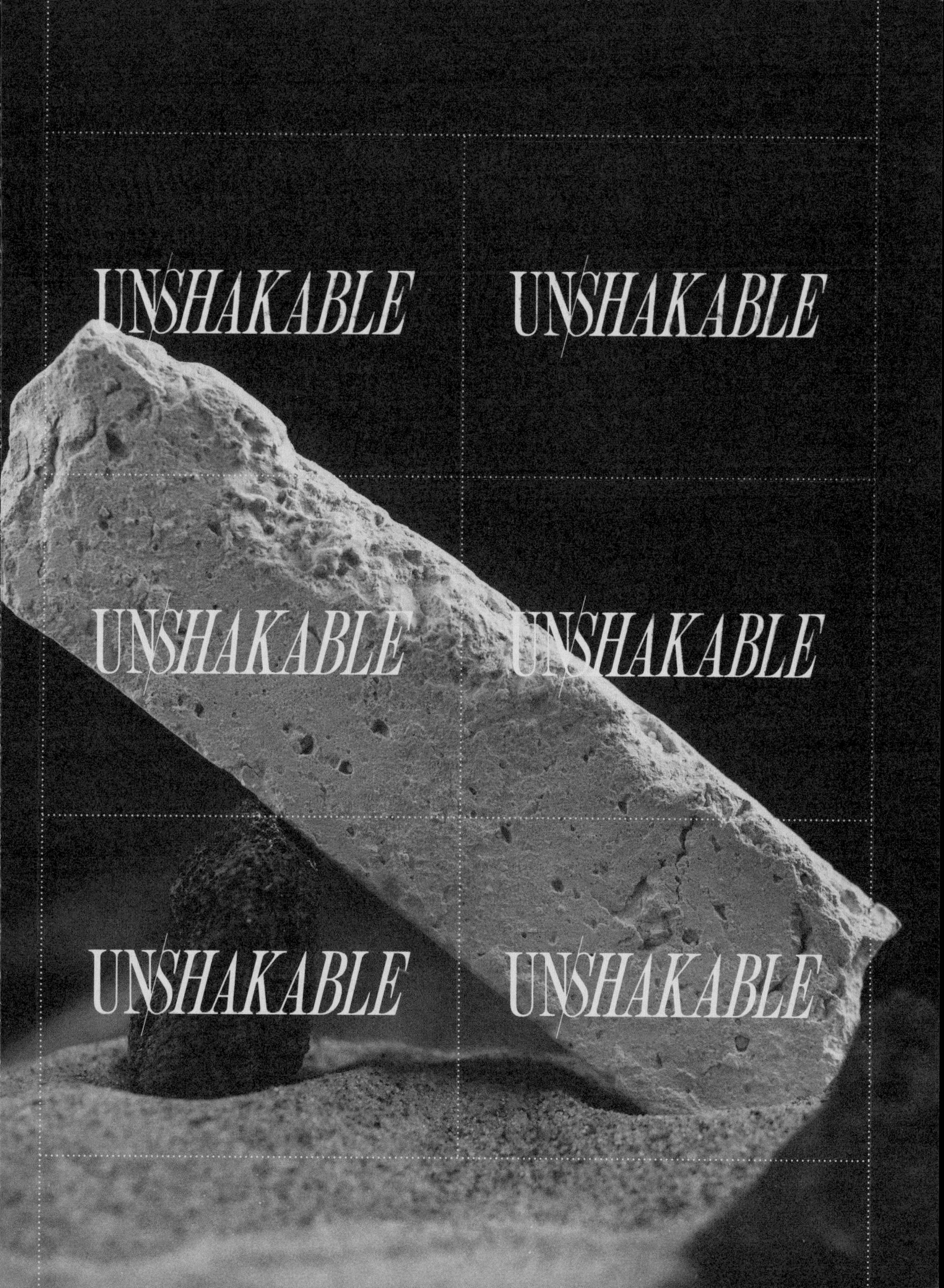
UNSHAKABLE
UNSHAKABLE
UNSHAKABLE
UNSHAKABLE
UNSHAKABLE
UNSHAKABLE

PSALM 62:1-2 (NIV)

1 Truly my soul finds rest in God; my salvation comes from him.
2 Truly he is my rock and my salvation; he is my fortress, I will never be shaken.

UNSHAKABLE · INTRO WEEK 1

PSALM 103:19 (NIV)

The Lord has established his throne in heaven, and his kingdom rules over all.

UNSHAKABLE · INTRO WEEK 2

PSALM 47:8 (NIV)

God reigns over the nations; God is seated on his holy throne.

UNSHAKABLE · WEEK 1

1 PETER 1:8 (NIV)

Though you have not seen him, you love him; and even though you do not see him now, you believe in him and are filled with an inexpressible and glorious joy...

UNSHAKABLE · WEEK 2

1 CORINTHIANS 4:20 (NIV)

For the kingdom of God is not a matter of talk but of power.

UNSHAKABLE · WEEK 3

COLOSSIANS 3:13 (NIV)

Bear with each other and forgive one another if any of you has a grievance against someone. Forgive as the Lord forgave you.

UNSHAKABLE · WEEK 4

PHILIPPIANS 4:19 (NIV)

And my God will meet all your needs according to the riches of his glory in Christ Jesus.

UNSHAKABLE · WEEK 5

REVELATION 22:20 (NIV)

He who testifies to these things says, "Yes, I am coming soon."
Amen. Come, Lord Jesus.

UNSHAKABLE · WEEK 6

1 JOHN 4:11-12 (NIV)

[11] Dear friends, since God so loved us, we also ought to love one another. [12] No one has ever seen God; but if we love one another, God lives in us and his love is made complete in us.

UNSHAKABLE · WEEK 7

1 THESSALONIANS 5:11 (NIV)

Therefore encourage one another and build each other up, just as in fact you are doing.

UNSHAKABLE · WEEK 8

UNSHAKABLE UNSHAKABLE

UNSHAKABLE UNSHAKABLE

UNSHAKABLE UNSHAKABLE